Green Div

GROWING YOUR
TEA GARDEN

A COMPLETE BEGINNER'S GUIDE TO GROW THE HERBS AND
PLANTS YOU NEED FOR YOUR INFUSIONS AND TEAS

INCLUDING SEVERAL HEALTHFUL HERBAL RECIPES

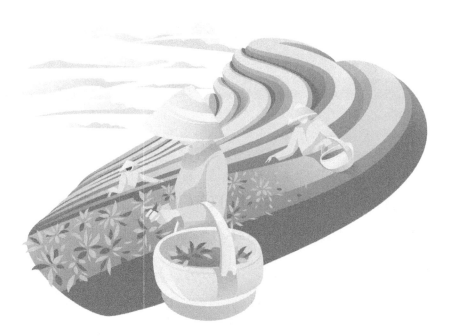

TABLE OF CONTENTS

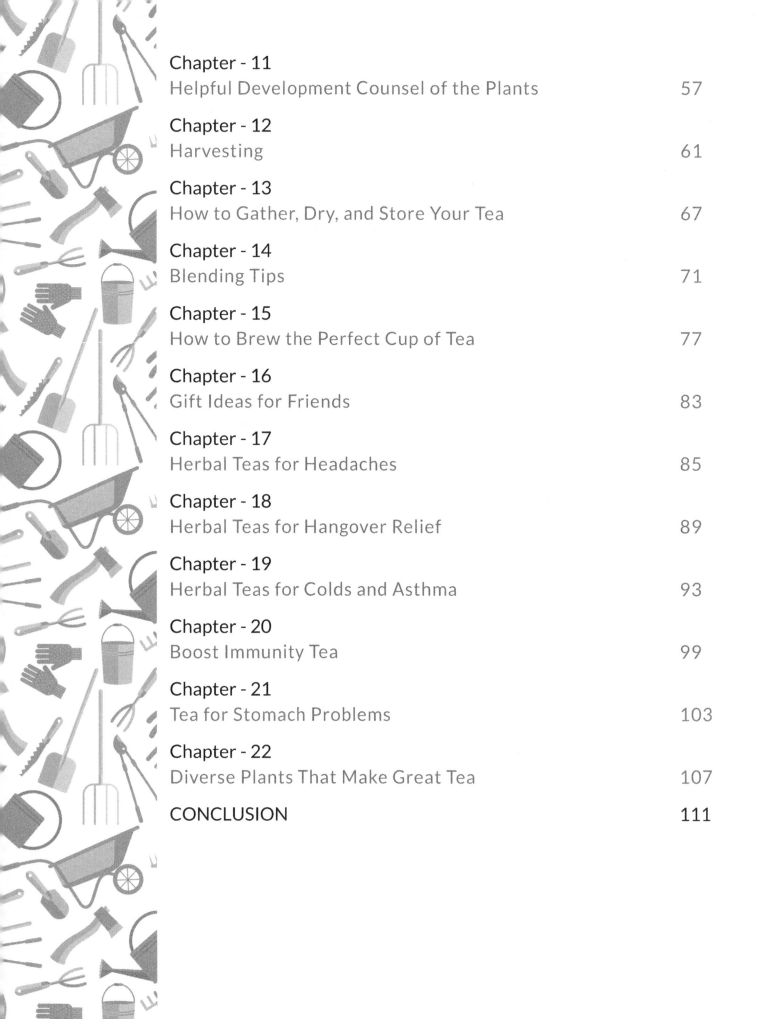

INTRODUCTION

I t is recommended to drink four to 6 cups of tea each day. If you can't get your hands on fresh tea leaves, then it is recommended that you should drink at least 3 cups. The benefits of tea are essentially the result of a group of substances called polyphenols, which are naturally occurring antioxidants. They have been shown to offer protection against cardiovascular disease and cancer while promoting overall immunity and slowing the aging process. Tea can also improve brain activity and mental clarity. Besides, all tea leaves are also loaded with minerals and vitamins.

1 cup of black tea contains about the same amount of caffeine as 1 cup of coffee; however, green tea contains about half the amount of caffeine per cup. Tea stimulates digestion and is vital for cleansing the colon. It is rich in fiber content which helps to treat constipation and other digestive tract disorders.

In addition to the health benefits mentioned above, tea can also help prevent tooth decay and eliminate bad breath. It also acts as an antibacterial and antiviral agent that helps to prevent the spread of certain diseases like colds and flu.

Teas range from green to black teas to oolong and white teas. The type you choose comes down to personal preference. In terms of flavor, green tea has the most astringent taste, followed by white tea and black tea. Black tea has a woodier taste, and green tea has a milder taste.

YOU CAN DECIDE TO GROW TEA IN YOUR GARDEN

A tea garden can be a beautiful place to spend your time. Some people might think it's a difficult task to grow tea, but, in reality, it is fairly simple and so rewarding. Tea gardens can provide you with many different health benefits and come with a fresh and beautiful aroma.

Watering your tea garden is more important than you think. Tea needs to be watered twice a day. The frequency depends on the amount of tea you want to grow, but watering once every alternate day should suffice if you have just a few pots. You can use either rainwater, tap water, or bottled water that has been treated with special chemicals to reduce the possibility of bacteriological contamination.

A tea garden can be constructed in many different ways, and there are several types that you can choose from. Firstly, you can choose to garden outside in a small vegetable patch or somewhere in the backyard. Another alternative is constructing your tea garden on a larger scale, containing plants of several species. This type of tea garden can be set up on the side of your house or even in your front yard.

A tea garden can contain many different types of plants, which can be used to create an aromatic and appealing environment for your guests. The aroma that is created from your garden will be something that everybody will enjoy.

It is recommended that you choose indirect sunlight for your garden as this will be the most suitable for the growth of the tea. Many people choose to grow a tea garden in the spring or summer as the fresh air will be refreshing and clean.

Tea gardens may also make your home look much more beautiful by growing it in a very interesting way. For example, you can plant the leaves of the tea plants over your deck or patio to make it appear like a miniature landscape.

A small garden contains only about three hundred plants, whereas a large garden can contain up to nine thousand different varieties. In terms of soil acidity and alkalinity, the leaves are considered best watered with calcareous water, alkaline.

To cultivate a beautiful tea garden, you must start by obtaining tea seeds which can be found in some specialty tea stores. Some of the organizations are committed to distributing such seeds all over the world. These seeds can be planted into small pots and then later transplanted to larger ones as they grow.

The ideal environment for the growth of these plants is in temperate climates with warm summers and cold winters, and slightly acidic soil. They are also planted in areas with an annual rainfall of at least thirty inches and have good drainage. When growing your tea plants, the most important thing is to ensure that you get good-quality viable seeds.

Chapter - 1
HISTORY AND TRADITION

Once an exclusive luxury of the Chinese Emperors, tea was introduced to Europe in 1615 by Dutch traders. In 1664 King Charles II of England was served tea for the first time in London and it became all the rage among European nobility. Tea gardens were planted extensively throughout England and Holland to satisfy their newfound love for this beverage.

At first, tea was considered to be a medicinal plant, and beverages made from it could only be sold as medicine. The tea plant was not known in Europe as a beverage until the end of the 17th century.

In 1839, Robert Fortune began trading in tea and set up many English tea gardens in India. As the tea trade increased, it became clear that there was a serious shortage of quality leaves in England. At this time most tea consumed by Europeans was from China. Tea plants were harvested at their peak and sent to England where they would be dried and sold. When the demand increased for more and better teas of the highest quality, the entire process had to be repeated. The plants would be harvested several times through the year, but much of that production went unused.

In 1883, an Englishman named William Wills arrived in India and produced high-quality tea for the British market. His tea was a turbocharged version of formerly known varieties. Wills' tea was a soft, white pekoe that became known as fine or Bombay tea.

By 1888 the market had reached its saturation level and the quality of that was gone forever. The British company, Brooke Bond, replanted tea trees in Assam and produced a new tea for the European market: Ceylon tea.

In 1900 Wills introduced the Kapengkins of Assam to his techniques of labor-intensive harvest methods. The Kapengkins were also known by the name Palashs and were the most sought-after type of tea in England. This new breed of tea thrived in Assam and it was spread naturally to other regions of the world.

Teahouses were first built in China during the 3rd century. Emperor Chao wrote a book about how to grow, pick, and brew tea. This book led to the introduction of tea plantations by the Chinese. In the west, tea gardens were first built in the foothills of Nepal. Tea gardens then began to be built in India, Sri Lanka, and other countries around the world.

However, in Hong Kong, the first tea garden was built in 1880.

By 1886, there were over 40 tea gardens. Tea was an important crop in Hong Kong. Tea gardens covered almost half of the area of Hong Kong's new territories. During the First and Second World Wars, many tea gardens suffered widespread destruction because of their proximity to the Japanese and German front lines during battles. However, many were able to recover and rebuild after the war with help from Mainland China and Taiwan. However, in the 1950s and 1960s, many of Hong Kong's tea gardens were destroyed to make way for housing. The last major tea garden to be built in Hong Kong was Wong Nai Chung on Lantau Island. It was completed in 1970 and originally covered an area of 50 hectares. However, it was then reduced to less than 40 hectares after land reclamation in the 1990s. The government has demolished it.

In Japan, tea cultivation began in the year 1191 when a Zen Buddhist monk named Myoan Eisai traveled to China on pilgrimage and discovered that grown tea there was much better than what could be found in Japan at that time. In the Sengoku period (1467–1603), the development of tea cultivation accelerated and became the most important agricultural crop in Japan. Japanese took to tea drinking with enthusiasm during this time, and the Japanese tea ceremony was developed. Soon after the Meiji Restoration of 1868, Japan's

farmers began planting new tea plants in Japan for its consumption.

The history of tea gardening in Japan dates back to the 18th century when Japanese monks would cultivate plants to help them maintain a spiritual connection with nature. These monks viewed themselves as gardeners and artisans of their trees, harvesting and brewing tea for their use and gifts to other people.

Japanese tea gardens in general were not designed with aesthetics in mind; they were developed as an intrinsic part of spiritual practice. The natural beauty that is found in a Japanese garden is not created but rather discovered. When the garden's design allows for its surroundings to shape the garden, it becomes a reflection of them. This allows someone to focus not on the artistry of the landscape but rather on nature. This idea of finding your surroundings in a Japanese garden is called "Yokoi-ni" which means looking at the scenery through the garden.

Early 20th century tea cultivation in Japan was characterized by small farms owned by families who cultivated tea for domestic consumption. The first wave of commercial cultivation began in the late 19th century when the Japanese government started to import seeds from China and Taiwan to diversify crops. In these gardens, there were many various gardens of certain plants such as the "Kuki" variety, which was popular at that time but is now rarely grown. There were also small gardens of bushes and trees. Small tea trees of Chinese origin were planted in the early 20th century by government initiatives.

During this time, the second wave of tea cultivation was characterized by large plantations and the introduction of new varieties. Large plantations, usually owned by large corporations, specializing in a particular variety of tea they felt would be popular with customers. The planters would usually take cuttings from these plants to produce new seedlings for their use or sell them to other planters for cross-breeding purposes.

Because of the plantation farming nature of tea cultivation in Japan, it was usually done on a large, industrial-scale by people with little understanding of the plant. These plantations were very large and covered many hectares and replaced the former practice of cultivating small bushes. The use of fertilizers also increased during this period.

Because of these factors, many scholars feel that Japanese tea cultivation has suffered from a lack of traditional knowledge. Tea gardens began to be abandoned in the 1960s and 1970s as tea became more industrialized and mechanized. The small farms that were initially established during the Meiji Era (1868–1912) gradually migrated to large, commercial plantations during the 20th century. This trend continued until the 1970s when it lost favor with tea drinkers.

Japanese tea cultivation has come back into the limelight in recent years under the leadership of Noritoshi Yokoyama, who has been credited with reviving the tradition of Japanese tea cultivation and making it popular again.

The tea plants in these gardens were grown without fertilizer and had to adapt to their environment. The cultivation of wild plants is not a recent trend in Japanese culture. The first use of wild plants was during the Jomon Era about 10,000 years ago when people began to use wild plants as food. During the Sengoku Era in Japan, people began to understand some of the properties of plant life such as herbs, shrubs, and trees. This resulted in the use of tea plants being improved throughout the 16th, 17th, and 18th centuries.

The importance of tea plants during this period of Japan began to increase during the Edo Period. During this time, new tea seeds were brought from China in 1612 by Japanese traders who introduced them to Japan. Such people also influenced tea cultivation as the monk Gennin Nyodo visited China during the latter part of his life. During his time in China, Nyodo learned about the importance of growing tea plants from wild trees. He returned to Japan and officially began the cultivation of tea plants.

Tea plants were cultivated in Japan because it was believed that tea could be grown in any environment. Tea reproduction could also occur naturally because the seeds could be scattered by the wind, birds, or other animals. The demand for tea in Edo (now Tokyo) increased during the 17th century as people became wealthier due to trade with China. Furthermore, in the 17th century, higher demand for tea resulted from Daimyo being given tea supplies as a reward for their service to the shogun.

Around this time, Japan's ruling classes began to drink tea. Before then, only Buddhist monks and upper-class citizens could enjoy drinking tea. The rest of the population was not able to afford it. The tea ceremony

was introduced to Japan by nun Eisai, a monk from China who was well-versed in Zen Buddhism. The first teacher of the Japanese tea ceremony was Takeno Bikan, a Chinese monk based in Kyoto, Japan. Although he taught neither Japanese nor Chinese monks the tea ceremony, it spread throughout Japanese society nonetheless.

The art of brewing tea originated from China and spread through Asia during the Tang Dynasty (618–907). It is generally agreed that the art of tea drinking originated in China, and was adopted by Japan during the Heian period (794–1185); however, the precise origins of this crucial practice are unknown.

The Gongoro, a boiling water method for making tea using boiling stones, was developed by Buddhist monks in 994 AD. In 1191 AD, the Zen monk Eisai introduced brewing tea in Japan. His steeping tea leaves in hot water were the first known method of brewing tea as we know it today. He also brought back seeds and bushes of tea from his travels to China, India, and Bhutan.

The traditional garden is designed to be a working Japanese Tea Garden based on the Zen philosophy of "Yokoi-ni" (looking at nature through the garden). The ancient Japanese understood that all gardens and landscapes were organic in their construction; this means they are subject to change. Mistakes and failures are expected during building a garden. The man who tends to a garden is not God, nor is he in charge of nature. He must work with nature, not against it.

The Japanese tea garden is a work of art in which the present is blended with the past to create an ideal harmonious blend of beauty, nature, and tranquility. A Japanese garden has a spiritual quality to it. It is a place where peace can be found, where one can absorb and enjoy nature's gifts. A Japanese tea garden is a place of beauty, harmony, and even some mystery.

Chapter - 2
TEA'S ANCIENT ORIGINS

The first known mention of tea came in ancient Chinese writings dating to the 3rd century BC. A book named Ch'a Ching, or Classic Book on Tea, was written by an unknown author. It discusses tea plants, their uses, and cultivation methods. It also gives some insight into the first Chinese tea trade. The book includes a topic that shares the same name as the plant, "ch'a," which means tea.

The first use of tea may have been for the prevention of fevers and other health conditions. Many ancient cultures used herbal infusions to ease aches and pains. They also used them as tonics, dietary aids, and remedies for illnesses. The Greeks were very interested in tea because many thought it would bring health benefits to those who consumed it. The Romans used tea as their main beverage, while the Chinese used it as a medicinal drink. The Chinese preferred black tea over green tea and were not interested in the herb until much later.

Some consider its origins in Greece. But it is generally accepted that tea first arrived in China from India and Persia during the Tang Dynasty (618–907). Chinese medicine uses many different plants; however, they are mostly used in tinctures for medicinal properties or medicines for ailments.

Chinese people have been drinking tea for thousands of years, but during the Tang Dynasty (618–906) drinking tea was considered a national pastime and was a symbol of hospitality.

The earliest recorded use of tea as a medicinal drink can be found in the medical text The Yellow Emperor's Inner Canon, which was compiled around 2700 BC.

According to Chinese legends, tea was discovered by the emperor Shen Nung when some leaves accidentally fell in boiling water. He tasted the water, found it delicious, and named it "cha."

Tea spread from China to Tibet in 642 AD, and then to Japan in about 800 AD. From there it spread to the Middle East and Europe.

Tea has been cultivated for more than 5,000 years, making it one of the oldest beverages cultivated by humans. Modern tea gardens usually consist of three or four rows of tea plants that are placed close together. These rows are spaced at 10-foot intervals to maximize the yield per acre. The plants come in varieties that produce orange pekoe, pekoe, souchong, and other black teas (with varying numbers of leaves) and green tea varieties.

Since the invention of mechanized tea picking in the mid-20th century, plantation owners have become common to harvest and process their teas and small-scale growers to sell premium teas directly from their gardens to consumers.

The most important events in the history of tea are:

Tea cultivation began in China more than 4,000 years ago. In China, tea cultivation began around the Yangtze River near the end of the second millennium BCE. Tea cultivation then spread to central China, where the best tea leaves were cultivated. Chinese farmers planted seeds from the tea plant near shrubs or trees to protect the young plants from wind and soil erosion. They also planted various types of trees in their gardens to act as attractants for birds and butterflies, which would help keep pests at bay. In addition, they planted a variety of bamboo around their gardens because of its natural resistance to insects and disease. These plants also served to stabilize the soil, as they could retain nutrients in their roots which would otherwise be leached away by water.

During the Tang Dynasty (618–907 CE), tea plants spread even further as farmers planted tea seeds together with plants that could protect them from frost and flammability. Tea plants grew between staked bamboo shoots. Tea farming spread to the rest of China and tea production became an important industry for the country.

Tea was first introduced to Japan from China in 607 CE, after Atsukado-in, a Japanese Buddhist monk is said to have traveled on the back of an ox from India to China where he observed the planting and cultivation of tea in a small village by watching the monks drink green tea as part of their religious rituals. From the Japanese pronunciation of the word "cha", or tea, which is "cha-shi", eventually the Japanese changed their pronunciation of the word to "cha-no-yu".

Tea cultivation was introduced to Japan during the early Heian period (794–1185 CE) by Buddhist monks in China and became necessary for both monks and commoners alike. Within a few centuries, even women began working on tea plantations. At this time the tea plant was still very rare in Japan, and therefore called "he-cha" about the ocean; the leaves of this plant were put on the emperor's dinner table. As tea plantations began to be established in Japan, women were asked to work alongside male workers and take on jobs such as plucking leaves from a tree, drying them out, or making tea. In 1627, Japanese women working as tea pickers sued their employers for unfair pay and went on strike. This minor strike lasted four months and during that time, women's tea production decreased while men's production increased.

Tea and religion have long been intertwined in Japanese culture. Tea ceremonies were held every spring at shrines and temples, where people would pay respect to the gods with a tea ceremony. On Shinto holidays such as Tanabata, people would also drink tea to celebrate the gods and their romantic relationship with each other.

During the Edo period (1603–1867 CE), when Tokugawa Ieyasu came into power, the government dictated that all women and children worked on tea plantations. Upper-class women and children from wealthy families were also expected to work on the tea plantations for about a month out of every year, although this often was not enforced. Men and women worked separately on the plantation with men engaged in more strenuous physical labor such as fertilizing fields, burning stalks after harvest season, and handpicking tea leaves.

By the middle of the Edo period, some landowners began to move their tea plantations to the hillsides to grow tea in direct sunlight. This method was more efficient because it allowed for easier picking of tea leaves and improved tea quality. Other landowners continued growing tea on flat land by using shade covers. This method creates a stronger, less bright flavor since the leaves are shielded from direct sunlight.

During the Edo period, many new kinds of tea became popular and were often consumed in "ryokan", a type of Japanese inn. Tea became a luxury that only women from wealthy families were able to enjoy. Upper-class women took the time out of their busy lives to practice certain arts such as "Ikebana" (flower arranging) and "Chado" (the traditional Japanese tea ceremony).

The earliest documentation of tea production in India dates back to the 6th century CE. The Chinese tea production was first introduced to the south Indian ports of Thane and Chikmagalur in the 17th century.

For tea to be produced in India, certain regions must meet very specific conditions that include a cool climate and hot muggy summers. These conditions are found along the western coast of Tamil Nadu near Mayiladuthurai, Thanjavur, and Nagapattinam.

Tea plantations in India are not as big as those in China and Japan, but they are still an important part of the Indian economy. The major production of tea in India is located along the Western Ghats mountain range. This region has a cool climate that allows for leaves to be picked at a younger age than other places. For leaves to be used for tea production, they must be picked no more than three years after their cultivation. The use of earlier harvested leaves creates a very dull and bland flavor, so the leaves must be picked at the correct time.

The plucking of tea leaves is done by hand by small groups of women. The leaves are then processed into the tea using more manual labor in factories located in the same areas as the plantations. In India, 96% of tea production is done by less than 25 acres in size. These smaller areas produce about 57% of all tea production in India.

Tea in India is produced both organically and through the use of chemicals. The main pesticides used in India are copper sulfate and potassium organosulphate (both banned in food use in the EU). Consequently, for every kilogram of black tea produced, 50 kg. of chemical fertilizer and 10 kg. of pesticide are used. In 2006, Indian tea exports were worth USD 237 million.

In the United States, tea production is concentrated in two states: South Carolina and North Carolina. Each state produces over 200 million pounds of tea per year.

Tea production in the United States began in the early 16th century when Chinese laborers first brought tea plants to plantations. The first official American tea plantation was founded in 1699 at Assam, now situated within the Indian state of Assam, a region skilled in cultivating and processing such products. By 1794, there were 27,000 acres (110 km.) of planted tea across America. 5 years later, a disastrous hurricane struck the colonies, resulting in thousands of deaths and destroying many plantations. Today, the tea industry employs nearly two hundred thousand people, with the most successful plantations still staying under the ownership of descendants of those who first planted them.

The main areas for tea production in the US are South Carolina and North Carolina. The largest growing regions are estimated to be located near Charlotte and Charleston. Large amounts of tea are produced in these areas, with over 10 million pounds coming from just the Charleston area and 2 million pounds from Charlotte alone.

Tea production in the United States is also seen as a means of economic development through aid to less developed economies that cannot afford to produce their own. During World War II, tea production was deliberately curtailed by Washington to maximize the supply for the war effort.

Chapter - 3
NUTRITIONAL AND MEDICINAL BENEFITS OF TEA

Tea is found in most households, throughout the world. It is rich in antioxidants and drinkers are advised to incorporate it into their diet due to its many health benefits.

HEALTH BENEFITS OF GREEN TEA

Green tea is a stimulant but consumed traditionally before bedtime it may help you sleep better and longer according to Traditional Chinese Medicine's belief in balanced Qi. Caffeine also stimulates metabolism which helps the body burn fat more efficiently while reducing sugar cravings. Green tea may also lower cholesterol and help the body ward off cancer and heart disease.

HEALTH BENEFITS OF BLACK TEA

Black tea has similar benefits to green tea, including reducing cholesterol and lowering heart disease risks, and being rich in antioxidants, which can help ward of cancer and infections. Black tea also contains vitamin C, K, folate, potassium, and manganese. Some black teas contain up to three times the amount of flavonoids found in green teas. Black tea is thought to improve mental alertness and concentration when taken in moderation. You can even find a variety of health benefits for black tea on the web.

HEALTH BENEFITS OF WHITE TEA

White tea is made from immature plant buds and is pluck and dried without fermentation or oxidization. It is also rich in antioxidants. Besides the health benefits of black tea, white teas have been indicated to help improve cholesterol levels while reducing the signs of aging. The natural ingredients found in white tea help boost your immune system cells weakened by sun exposure, stress, or poor diet.

NUTRITIONAL BENEFITS OF TEA

Tea is rich in antioxidants, minerals and is a source of many vitamins including folate or folic acid. There is no fat or cholesterol in tea but it does contain some caffeine, most of which is found in the less popular varieties. Caffeine has been found to help fight cancer and lower blood pressure with no side effects. Tea also contains several minerals, including potassium, calcium, iron, and magnesium, often lacking in diets. 1 cup of tea can provide over 100% of the recommended daily intake of zinc. Tea is also a great foil to water and can help you stay hydrated for long periods.

Tea and Weight Loss

Drinking tea may help you lose weight, provided that you drink it regularly. Tea contains zero fat and is rich in water so it fills the stomach without adding calories. Catechins in tea have been found to promote a sense of fullness. In addition, tea is rich in antioxidants which promote a healthy heart and immune system. Tea consumption is also associated with a lower risk of obesity and diabetes.

Tea and Diet

Being rich in monounsaturated and polyunsaturated fats, tea helps reduce cholesterol levels and promotes a healthy heart. Tea is also low in calories, making it a great alternative to sugar-filled sodas, which can rack up

many empty calories. It is quite nutritious so 1 cup can provide you with just about all the essential nutrients except fat, iron, and protein.

Antioxidants in tea can also help hinder damage to your DNA and inhibit the development of cancer cells. Tea, especially green tea, may also help prevent certain types of cancer, including breast and ovaries.

Green tea is best consumed in moderate amounts as it has caffeine which can interfere with sleep. Black tea is best avoided if you have stomach or digestive irritations since it contains tannins that may worsen symptoms. White tea is the safest and least popular type of tea since it contains no caffeine or tannins. White tea contains a compound called epigallocatechin, which effectively inhibits diabetes, helping to reduce blood pressure and improve cholesterol. It also appears that white tea can reduce the risk of developing breast cancer by as much as 90%.

The acidity of tea might help reduce the risk of some types of cancer and heart disease by neutralizing the harmful effects of certain free radicals. A study conducted by the University of Oxford concluded that tea may have a protective effect against breast cancer.

A study conducted at the University of California in Riverside found that drinking up to 2 cups of green tea a day was associated with a reduced risk of heart disease.

Tea and Bone Health

1 cup of green tea can supply you with over 50% of your daily calcium needs. The vitamin C, potassium, and other nutrients in white or oolong teas may help improve bone mineral density and reduce broken bones.

Tea and Oral Health

One study in the American Journal of Clinical Nutrition found that drinking 4–5 cups of green tea a day can help prevent tooth decay. Drinking green tea has been found also to improve bad breath. A study published in the Journal of the American Dental Association found that daily consumption of green tea may help relieve gingivitis.

Tea and Your Skin

Consumption of tea has been associated with better hydration and it may help prevent dry skin, eczema, rashes, and age spots. Green tea is also good for your hair and can help stimulate healthy hair growth. Drinking green tea will also improve your complexion since it contains antioxidants that will leave you looking more youthful.

The antioxidants present in tea may help fight skin pollution to help slow down the aging process. Due to its high content of zinc and polyphenol antioxidants, tea can also help you look younger.

Tea and Your Mood

Green tea is full of L-theanine which has been found to have anti-stress effects and increase alertness. L-theanine has also been found to have a relaxing effect on the body without the drowsiness associated with anti-depressants. Tea can also help you boost your mood by regulating hormones in the brain.

Tea and Longevity

The tea plant is believed to be one of nature's oldest, cultivated in China for thousands of years. Tea is an effective natural remedy for many conditions including diabetes, high blood pressure, and even cancer. Green tea has also been found to have anti-cancer properties and may inhibit tumor development. As a result, drinking green tea is thought to increase longevity which could provide significant advantages for older people.

Tea and Caffeine

Tea contains caffeine which is a known stimulant. The same effect caused by drinking coffee can also be felt after consuming tea, with many people getting an energy boost and feeling more awake after drinking green or white tea. However, too much caffeine can cause jitters and insomnia.

Tea leaves contain small amounts of theobromine which has similar properties to caffeine but with a milder effect. Caffeine is found in coffee, cocoa, cola, black tea, and some herbal teas. Tea contains more than twice as much naturally occurring caffeine as coffee.

Tea and Cancer

A study issued in the Journal of the American Medical Association found that drinking 3–5 cups of green tea a day may help prevent breast cancer. Green tea may also help protect against esophageal, bladder, colon, and prostate cancer by lowering blood sugar levels and helping to prevent abnormal cell growth.

Preventing cancer requires a combination of factors including not just a healthy diet and exercise but also stress reduction. Adding green tea to your daily routine may help improve your overall health and contribute to a longer life.

Tea and Inflammation

Either abnormal cell growth or inflammation causes nearly every disease. Research issued in the Journal of Allergy and Clinical Immunology found that drinking 4 cups of green tea per day could help reduce chronic inflammation associated with allergies.

Tea and Mental Health

Tea has been reported to be effective in improving concentration, aiding in dementia, depression, and anxiety.

The amino acids L-theanine and L-glutamate found in tea have been shown to improve focus and mood.

Studies show that theanine increases alpha brain waves, which means you will become mentally alert and calm without drowsiness. Theanine is also a mild Alpha-1/dopamine antagonist which means that it has the potential to improve cognition.

Theanine has been shown to improve mental performance in adults and children. The children with ADD (Attention Deficit Disorder) showed a statistically significant improvement in attention when they consumed theanine. Another study involving college students showed that theanine improved performance on vigilance tests, motor speed, perceptual learning, and memory.

NATURAL TEAS

Tea is one of the most popular drinks globally, and natural teas have been growing in popularity because they're healthier for you. Most commercial tea gardens use pesticides to maintain a perfect crop of green tea leaves, but more people are switching to organic or natural teas. These teas are grown in the wild, sometimes by ethnic people who have been growing them for generations.

The most common organic or natural teas are white, green, oolong, and black.

Natural green tea is the most popular. It can be purchased in many health food stores and available at many restaurants (tea bars). It comes in loose-leaf form and can be stored easily in a glass jar. It has a mild flavor and is very caffeine-free, which makes it the best choice for people who want to minimize their caffeine intake without missing out on the health benefits of tea.

Natural oolong tea is fermented, so it's a little bit more potent than green tea. It has a rich flavor and can be steeped multiple times. It is also caffeine-free.

Natural white tea is the least processed type of tea. It is made from the buds and leaves of young tea trees, and it takes years for these trees to fully mature. The flavor is sweet and floral, with a delicate aroma.

Natural black tea comes from fully grown tea trees. The leaves are withered and then oxidized to give the black color and strong taste that black teas are known for. The leaves are sun-dried, which gives them their characteristic flavor and aroma.

Growing your tea garden is a fun way to get more out of green tea and natural tea without spending a lot of money. You don't need to know anything about plants or green tea to grow your garden. Many people prefer growing their garden because it's much more economical than purchasing organic or natural teas in stores.

The different colors of natural teas come from the different processing used by organic farms in their respective regions.

Black organic tea from Darjeeling is probably the most popular variety of black organic tea in the world. It's strong and bold, like a black tea but with a hint of cinnamon and nutmeg.

Natural teas are often called wild teas because they're not grown in plantations or factories, but instead by people who harvest and process the leaves grown by their neighbors. This is a very different process than factory-grown teas, which are harvested in the early morning when the dew has evaporated.

One of the most popular kinds of natural tea is black tea, which comes from China and is processed to create a smooth-drinking black liquid. Making this tea is very different from green teas, which are withered or bruised and allowed to dry. Black tea is roasted after being rolled in a heated drum. The heat drives the moisture out of the leaves, and then they're fire-cured so that they never have contact with moisture.

The most popular black teas are Pouchong, whose leaves are rolled tightly into balls that unfurl when steeped; and Dian Hong, a black tea that's partially fermented and has an earthy taste. Famous natural teas from this region include Iron Goddess of Mercy, a black tea blended with cinnamon, orange peel, anise, and cloves; and Silver Needles, a white tea whose leaves are tipped with downy silver-white hairs.

Natural teas are also available in green form, including Dragonwells that are lightly fermented and light-tasting. Many Chinese green teas are scented with jasmine flower petals or sakura flowers. These teas are often sweetened with honey, cane sugar, or agave nectar.

While many people enjoy drinking natural teas, it's important to consider that these teas are grown in very different ways.

Chapter - 4
LEARN ABOUT THE PLANT THAT PRODUCES
WHITE, GREEN, OOLONG, AND BLACK TEAS

Tea is one of the most popular drinks globally, and for many of us, it's a morning ritual. But did you know that tea comes from a plant? Tea is cultivated from Camellia sinensis, producing white, green, oolong, and black teas.

Did you know that Camellia sinensis is a small shrub and not a tree? It might be hard to come by one of these plants in your area as they typically grow in subtropical climates like southern China or India. If you can find one though, keep it outside the colder months (October-April) where it's only cold tolerant to about 5 °C (23 °F).

Camellia sinensis is part of the Theaceae family, which encompasses 2,000 plant species. Camellia sinensis is an evergreen shrub that reaches about 1.5 m. (5 ft.) in height. It has small, semi-evergreen leaves with a sword shape and a white flower that develops into a small red berry that contains the seeds which are then collected for tea production.

Camellia sinensis is native to China and most commonly found in Zhejiang province. There are over a hundred named cultivars of tea plants that affect the way the tea is processed. For example, depending on foliage growth, a plant can be classified as either an Assamese or Kenyan variety. The Chinese refer to the variation as Wuyi or Fujian types, respectively.

Camellia sinensis is either propagated by seed or via cuttings from a mother plant (cutting propagation). A tree is planted when the young plant reaches about 2–3 m. (6–9 ft.). The mature plants are about 5 m. (16 ft.) tall.

Plants growing in the wild can be found up to an altitude of 1,200 m. (about 3,900 ft.). It is only found in subtropical regions. This is because it needs many moisture and clouds to grow due to its semi-evergreen leaves and short growing season.

This plant is easily bred because it can be grown from seed indoors or in containers with minimal cold

hardiness issues. One advantage of growing Camellia sinensis indoors is that the indoor environment mimics that found in a subtropical climate.

Once the plant has reached about 1.5 m. (5 ft.) in height, it can be propagated easily from cuttings and transplanted to a new location or used for shade and ornamentation of a patio or yard.

One of the best ways to use this plant as an ornamental is to graft it onto existing trees with rootstock. The grafting allows it to be grown from seed indoors or in containers that will grow outdoors and the existing rootstock.

Camellia is a hardy plant that can be grown in areas that are too cold for other plants. Still, it needs enough moisture and moisture retention, especially during colder months between October and April. It gets more susceptible to frost than deciduous trees and shrubs.

The plants start to flower during the summer months and produce small red berries ($\frac{1}{2}$–1-inch in diameter) edible. The tea is produced when these red berries are fermented, dried, and later roasted. Camellia sinensis gets its unique taste profile from numerous factors including soil composition, water levels, tea processing time, harvest time, and storage time, and how often the plant has been fertilized.

This small shrub can be used as a hedge (pruning is needed but not difficult). It can be used as an ornamental plant and as a cover for a yard so that other plants can take root. Pruning is needed to maintain plants at the desired height.

When the new growth starts to yellow, it is pruned to one to two pairs of leaves (this promotes an even flush of new growth) and later left unpruned so that the plant can produce tea.

UNDERSTANDING THE DIFFERENCES BETWEEN BLACK TEA, GREEN TEA, WHITE TEA, AND HERBAL TEA

There are four main types of tea: black, green, white, and herbal iced teas. Each type differs in processing and color due to changes in oxidation levels caused by variations in temperature when fermented or dried from their fresh state. There are also differences in the way they are harvested and processed. Black tea is fermented and then oxidized. Black is the least processed tea. Green and white teas are made by steaming or pan firing, which preserves the leaves. White tea usually has a lighter, more flowery flavor than green or black teas. Herbal iced teas are made by infusing flavors into the leaves before drying them, in addition to using a steeping method that results in a stronger herbal tea flavor.

Regardless of type, all teas contain the same biochemical components. They are powerful antioxidants that have many health benefits, such as helping to reduce heart disease and cancer.

- **Black tea:** Black tea is fully oxidized during processing. This gives it a dark color and bolder flavor

than green or white tea, which are not oxidized. It also contains higher levels of the caffeine compound, although this can be reduced using less water when steeping it. However, many people believe that black tea provides the greatest health benefits because it is oxidized. It is then often sold as "oolong," "black" or "red" tea; however, true oolong and red teas are completely oxidized during processing and do not contain any fully un-oxidized tea leaves.

- **Green tea:** Green tea is partially oxidized, or "green." It is picked by hand before it becomes fully oxidized. It contains the highest levels of antioxidants of all teas, contributing to it having a multitude of health benefits.

- **White tea:** White tea is fully oxidized during processing; it can be yellow but will always be white. It also contains significant levels of caffeine, although less than black, and can affect your body faster than other types of tea. It has a light flavor without the smoky taste of black tea.

- **Herbal tea:** Many herbal teas on the market are tisanes, or herbal infusions, instead of true teas. They are steeped in hot water with fresh or dried herbs but not fully oxidized. Therefore, they are not technically teas, but they still provide a variety of health benefits. Herbal teas are restricted to certain types of herbs, so make sure to check the ingredients before you buy them.

DON'T BUY STORE-BOUGHT BLENDS WHEN HOMEGROWN IS SO MUCH BETTER!

Tea is a wonderful beverage. It's been enjoyed for centuries and it can be paired with just about any cuisine. But did you know that a tea garden also makes for an excellent hobby?

You can grow your tea and have complete control of the tea's quality.

With your garden, you can choose what kind of plants to grow and how many to plant. You can also select the varieties of tea plants you prefer. With your garden, you can get ultra-fresh tea leaves.

The cost of tea can vary depending on the season as well as the quality. Therefore, you will not get bored with the taste of your tea because you can grow different plants and select different varieties. Your children will learn about nature.

Growing your garden helps you connect with nature because you will be able to observe it close up. Not only that, they get to help in taking care of the plants as well as picking out them when they reach maturity.

However, you need to be aware that growing your tea plants is not easy. You would need to do a few things, like picking out the seeds and planting them, watering the plants on time, and pruning. But these are all part of the fun.

You can also learn how to create your compost so that you can fertilize your plants easily. You also need to know how to harvest the leaves because this will determine your tea's quality. If you know how to do it, you will maintain your plants and make sure that they are healthy.

You can also decide on the right time to plant your plants because the main objective of growing your tea is to have a great tasting tea and if you have the techniques for growing, this will be easy.

When you start harvesting your leaves, make sure that you pick them when they are fresh. Otherwise, they may have mildew and fungus which can contaminate the tea leaves. You can also try to dry them even more so that you can store them for later consumption. After harvest, you need to store the seeds properly and keep them dry.

One of the most crucial factors in growing your tea is fertilizing. This is because many factors determine how fast a plant grows, whether it is healthy or excess rainfall. Since you are using these fertilizers which have been created either by nature or by you, they should not cause any harm to your plants.

Teaching your children the importance of nature is an important aspect as well. Once they learned how to grow their tea, you can easily show them how to care for it.

Another reason to have a garden is that you can simply let the vegetables grow by themselves and let them be fresh and organic because they will not require too much effort on your part.

This may be new for you but once you start growing your tea, it will be fun, easy, and exciting. Since you will be able to harvest your tea, you can also have a lot of fun trying out different recipes that call for tea leaves.

GROWING YOUR OWN TEA GARDEN ALSO HAS SOME OTHER ADVANTAGES

Growing your tea is a fun and rewarding hobby. But don't just take our word for it:

- The tea you grow yourself will be fresher, more flavorful, and less expensive than what you can buy in a store.

- You can control the quality of ingredients used in your tea plant's diet. Many commercial teas are fertilized with pesticides to keep them alive in their natural environment outside, but all the fertilizers are done by hand when grown indoors.

- Unlike most flowers, tea plants make great houseplants and can be taken with you if you move or have to live overseas for a few years.

- Growing your tea gives you and your family an unusual hobby, both time-consuming and rewarding.

- You will have access to high-quality ingredients that can be used to cook dishes for yourself or your

friends.

- Growing your tea with children is an excellent way to teach them responsibility, science, math, and how to take care of their possessions.

- Growing your tea is a rewarding hobby that will have enriching benefits for you and your family.

- Growing your tea can allow you to learn new skills, such as growing various herbs or plants in containers.

- Growing your tea will allow you to create a more interesting and relaxing environment by adding live plants and flowers.

- You may be able to sell any excess teas you have grown for a profit. Growing your tea is usually more profitable than taking cuttings from other people's plants.

- Learning how to grow your tea is a skill and accomplishment for you to be proud of.

- Growing your tea allows you to experiment with new herbs, blending various varieties in your tea.

ADVANTAGES OF GROWING TEA FOR SELLING/PROFESSIONAL PURPOSES

- Teas are a competitive market and have been earning profits of up to $6 per pound.

- Tea plants can be grown indoors in pots, so you do not need a large garden area.

- You can grow your tea from seed or take cuttings from other's plants to sell.

- The initial costs for starting a tea garden are minimal since many supplies can be reused.

- Growing your tea gives you access to a unique and profitable item to sell.

- You will become familiar with the plant and its needs, which can help you provide better customer service.

- Teas are an unusual plant to grow in your home or garden; this can set you apart from other gardeners or florists in your area.

- Children can become familiar with growing their tea and will learn the value of money.

- You can grow other herbs and plants to go inside your pots with your tea plants, creating a beautiful environment for yourself.

Chapter - 5
GROWING TEA

If you're interested in growing your tea, you probably already enjoy tea and know a little bit about it. However, if you haven't already done so, take the time to read this book on growing tea before getting started with your garden. Several things will help you grow a healthy and fruitful crop; knowing the basics is an excellent way to start. Find out whether or not there are local growers who sell high-quality plants or seedlings.

You might also want to start a journal of your garden's progress. Include information about how it's doing during different seasons, what you want to grow, what kind of fertilizer you want to use, and which plants thrive while others are dying off. Start with the basics like soil type and sun exposure; you'll need to know if your plants are receiving enough sunlight or if they're remaining too wet or dry.

GROWING YOUR OWN TEA GARDEN

Growing your tea garden can be fun and rewarding if you have a green thumb. The most popular tea varieties are black, green, white, oolong, and rooibos. Still, some plants produce teas outside these traditional categories like the blueberry bush with its berry-flavored leaves. The main prerequisites for growing your tea garden are a sunny location with well-drained soil, adequate water, and a bit of patience. The good news is that many plants used in tea gardens grow well in containers. It is an excellent way to add some green to your life without taking up too much space. In a couple of years, the plants will outgrow their containers and you can sell them for a profit. With proper care, there's no limit to what you can grow. You can garden indoors, especially if your home is warm or has excellent air conditioning but even when life is comfortable, nothing beats the fresh air in nature. Large cities and suburbs are often overlooked as suitable locations for tea gardens because of their artificial nature but with some planning and ingenuity, new possibilities are nearly endless.

Please note: Be sure to check the requirements for your specific plant before you decide which one to buy.

Some need more sunlight than others or different amounts of water or fertilizer. The amount of water it needs depends, of course, on its specific needs and the amount of sunlight it receives. A plant's growth will also depend on the temperature in your garden or container. For example, a blueberry bush will grow well at temperatures between 40–80 °F.

Growing your tea garden can be cheap and simple. Many varieties of plants used to make tea are perennial, meaning they survive year after year, so you don't have to start from scratch every spring. These plants can be grown in a wide range of conditions so you can grow them in almost any climate. To ensure healthy growth, most require rich soil with plenty of nutrients but not too much nitrogen (as too much nitrogen will produce rapid but weak growth. If your soil is poor, you can amend it with compost or manure. If you are using a container and don't have access to good soil, buy some potting soil from a nursery. If you live in a temperate climate, aim for a spot where the temperature stays around 65 °F during the day and no lower than 45 °F at night. If you live in a warmer climate, plant your tea garden in the shade.

INFORMATION YOU NEED TO PLAN AND PLANT A HEALTHY GARDEN

A little less than a hundred years ago, the first tea gardens were planted over what had been virgin land. This was a watershed event for the tea industry.

This is all about how you can grow your tea garden, and how you can get started in this rewarding hobby of "tea gardening."

Here are some pointers to help you plan and plant your new garden:

- Tea gardens can be plain or ornamental depending on which plants are used. Ornamental gardens usually provide fragrance as well as visual interest.

- The core of any good garden is the soil, so start with the soil and work your way around.

- Choose a site for your garden that is in full sun or has some shade, but does not have an overbearing breeze.

- The best time to plant a new tea garden is after spring frost and before summer drought. In other words, while the weather is not too hot or too dry.

- Plant a tea garden in an area that is 1x1 m. (2.5x2.5 ft.) in size or larger, but not larger than 2x2 m. (6x6 ft.).

- If you are going to grow more than one variety of tea plants, this is the time to plan your variety bed. Start by planting 3 plants of the same type or choose a single plant and add more when it produces buds.

- If you want to grow your tea, be sure to ask for the bud and a few leaves from a friend who already has

a garden.

- Plant your tea bed at least 30 cm. (1 ft.) apart or about 1 m. (3 ft.) if you have the area. This will give you room to maintain your garden without damaging the plants. Remember that some plants like to be planted close, while others need more room. When in doubt, use the larger spacing.

- A compost pile should be added to your tea garden, and the heap should be kept moist. Compost is the best fertilizer for most plants. If you do not have a pile already, start one now. Do not add meat or dairy products to the compost.

- Once you have planted your garden, keep it well weeded for the first few years until all of your plants are well established.

- Select a tall or large variety of plants to act as a "leader," and tuck more plants behind it.

- A tea garden needs protection from the hot afternoon sun, so consider adding a trellis or umbrella to your garden for an extra level of shade. Your plants will thank you for it.

- If you are planting another row of plants behind your leader, space them at least 30 cm. (1 ft.) apart.

- Once you have planted your tea garden and it is established, you will probably need to provide additional fertilizer. Calcium is the most important ingredient in tea plants. In fact, calcium deficiency can be a major problem for tea plants. Tea plants like to have a regular dose of calcium for their health and growth.

HOW TO PLANT SOME OF THE MORE POPULAR TISANES AND TEAS

The best way to grow your own tea garden is by planting some of the most popular tisanes and tea types.

How to Plant Some of the More Popular Tisanes

Plant tisanes in a shady spot where they will receive partial sunlight that is well-drained. Many people think they can just plant them in regular soil, but you will have much better growth and health if you use a potting mix made for tropical plants.

They like rich soil with good drainage. Plant them after the danger of frost is past so the roots can establish themselves well before spring when new growth comes out.

- It's best to plant in areas with little foot traffic so the plants get more nutrients from the sun and rainwater.

- It's important to plant at the proper time of the year so that the plants are not stressed.

- The best time to plant them is in a few days after the new moon in August each year.

- They should be planted at a depth of 2.5 times the height of the quantity you want to grow. The soil needs to be heavily irrigated so that it drains well and properly aerates the soil.

- Plant in groups of three or more in different spots around your yard. The plants take some time to establish themselves but once they have rooted they will grow very fast.

- It is best to use living soil so that the plant can absorb the nutrients. It's best to use compost blended with fresh cow manure for rich and healthy soil. For larger plants, you can also add some coffee grounds.

- The tisanes will thrive in warmer temperatures and more sun. They will grow faster in the summer and they will not have to be watered as frequently. They are good plants for home gardens or fountains that are often watered.

How to Plant Some of the More Popular Teas

- Plant tea plants in a shady spot where they will receive partial sunlight that is well-drained. It's important to use a potting mix made for tropical plants so the roots will flourish.

- It's best to plant in areas with little foot traffic so the plants get more nutrients from the sun and rainwater. It's also important to plant at the proper time of the year so that the plants are not stressed and have time to establish themselves before spring comes around.

- It's best to plant them during the new moon in August each year.

- It's best to use soil that is living so that the nutrients can be absorbed by the plant. It's best to use compost blended with fresh cow manure for rich and healthy soil. For larger plants, you can also add some coffee grounds.

- Tea plants like warmer temperatures and more sun than other plants. They will thrive in warmer temperatures and more sun than other plants.

- The best time to plant them is during the new moon in August each year.

- It's important to plant them in groups of 3 or more in different spots around your yard. The plants take some time to establish themselves but once they have rooted they will grow very fast.

- You can plant them first and then add coffee grounds to the soil during planting so that it will help the plants get established.

- You can garden indoors or in a sunny window and transplant it into an open area when the weather cools down.

- You can grow these plants in containers or you can transplant them into a bigger pot.

- Home gardeners should be sure to use loamy soil and know how to propagate these plants.

- The main goal is to grow healthy and vigorous tea plants so that they don't die out during the winter season but will continue growing in the spring when temperatures rise again.

YOU CAN USE THE FOLLOWING METHOD TO GIVE YOUR PLANTS WHAT THEY NEED

1. Fill a bucket with 3 parts of well-rotted manure (night soil) and 1 part compost (night soil with kelp).

2. Use a trowel to apply the mixture liberally along the rows in your garden.

3. Water this well and continue watering every time you water your garden.

4. A few months after you begin providing calcium to your plants, you will start to see calcium deposits along the branches of your tea plants. This is a good indicator that you are on the right track.

5. Once or twice a year dust a layer of lime over the area around your plant stems and leaves. This will help reduce fungus in your garden.

6. If you are planning on growing more than one variety of tea plants in one garden, be sure to keep the plants separated. Some teas have a similar appearance to other varieties and can easily be mistaken for

another type. This could lead to disease or pests hitting your wrong plant.

7. After you have a few years of experience, consider getting together with like-minded tea growers. Make new friends and share plants, ideas, and stories about tea gardening with each other.

8. Many new tea gardeners think that their tea plants will be crowded if they are in a group. They do not realize that once the plants have grown and matured, you can cut back the growth of all of your plants to fit within the dimensions of your garden.

9. This is a great time to take out your shears and pruners and enjoy an early winter pruning in your tea garden to keep them tidy and compact. You can also remove any dead or dying plants in your garden.

10. Tea plants like to be planted close together, while others need more room. When in doubt, use the larger spacing.

When you think about it, tea is a member of the mint family and they all share one thing in common—they produce a leaf with a surface that is covered with tiny holes called "hairs" that trap carbon dioxide gas from the air and give the tea its distinctive aroma. These holes also allow the aroma to be released when you drink your tea.

Chapter - 6
HOW TO GROW YOUR TEA FROM SEEDS, CUTTINGS, OR SMALL PLANTS?

Tea plants in the garden benefit from plenty of sunlight but need shelter on chilly nights. They'll grow well if they are planted near taller plants that provide shade during the day and let the warm sunshine on them at night.

PREPARING THE SEEDS

Tea seeds should be sown on the surface of the soil, not into rows or drills in the place where you plan to grow them. If you use a seed tray that is designed to hold tea seeds there will probably be enough room for them to grow.

If you don't have a seed tray, then sow your tea seeds in well-drained soil in shallow containers such as jam jars or plastic boxes with drainage holes at the bottom.

If you sow the seeds into seed trays or another pot, they should be lightly covered with compost or soil.

If you are growing a few tea plants in a large container, you may have to thin them out so that each plant has enough space to develop properly. The container may already be too small when you buy it. In this case, it is best to take the tea plants out of their container and grow them in individual pots before planting them in the garden.

Steps:

1. When the weather is warm, take your tea seeds out of their prior container and wash them off so that their roots are free to develop.

2. Plant the seeds level with the surface of the soil but not too deep. This prevents them from rotting in the ground overnight.

3. Water your tea seeds regularly until you see signs of life, such as a few tiny leaves beginning to appear on

each seedling or a small root emerging from each seedling.

4. When your tea plant seedlings are large enough to handle, you can transplant them into individual pots. You need a pot that is about twice the size of the root system.

5. Place a layer of broken clay pots or coarse gravel at the base of the pot so that the roots can develop properly in good, well-drained soil.

TRANSPLANTING SEEDLINGS

Prepare your transplanting soil by adding compost and organic matter so that it is loose and light enough for young roots to grow through easily.

You can also provide extra protection from the sun by covering the pots with plastic or a blanket.

You cannot use a ready-made soil mix that includes peat moss or coir as it will cause tea plants to rot.

If you do not want to transplant your plants from the seedling stage, you can plant them into the ground in early spring next year after the last frost date.

Pots should be placed into holes drilled into garden beds at least 1-inch deep and 6-inch apart.

The roots will grow through the soil, developing strong stems.

Steps:

1. When the weather is warm, take your tea seeds out of their prior container and wash them off so that their roots are free to develop.

2. Carefully remove the pot from its former position and place it in a new hole at the same depth as it was in its earlier position so that the roots are at the same depth as they were when they were tiny seedlings.

3. Plant the seedling with the stem in water until it is larger.

4. After a few days, take the pot out of the hole and place it on some newspaper or other strong material so that the soil around it does not dry out.

5. When your tea plant has at least six leaves, take it out of the pot and plant it in separate pots that are also about half its size or less than half its size.

Native tea plants are usually very well adapted to tea cultivation and will grow in the wild, but they are also useful for quickly producing a robust starter garden of native species.

Growing native plants is similar to growing tea except that you should not use fertilizers rather than letting

them develop in compost or manure-based organic matter.

Tea plants can be propagated by taking cuttings of the stems in spring or summer.

There are also many different techniques for propagating tea plants.

You can erect a trellis on which to grow your plants, and you can train the plant up the trellis using branches that have been cut from the plant. You can also plant the shoots in pots, at least if they are young and tender enough to survive transplanting.

SMALL PLANTS

If you want to grow small plants, you can use a cold frame or other sunny situation.

A cold frame is a structure that provides shade at night but allows the sun to shine on plants all day long.

The cold frame should be set up during the first week of April when the weather is still mild but not so mild that it is not warm enough for your tea plants to thrive in it during the day.

Steps:

1. It is best to grow the plants in a cold frame for the first few weeks of their life, but you can also use individual pots to keep them under control or grow your tea plants in a greenhouse that is ideally heated so that the temperature remains around 60 °F (15.5 °C).

2. As soon as you see signs of growth, cover your plants with glass or polythene sheets. You want to protect them from frost and excessive sunlight at the same time.

3. When the cold frame is in place, you can start your tea plants and keep them in there during the first two months of their life.

4. In the third month, you can take them out and bring them inside to a sunny location where they will begin to grow more rapidly.

5. After you see signs of growth, it is best to bring the plants into a greenhouse where they will remain for many weeks until they are ready for their final move indoors.

6. Take the plants out of the cold frame and place them in a sunny spot.

7. Your purpose with this is to get them used to be outdoors, so you will need to leave them outside for a few weeks before you bring them inside.

8. After you have placed your tea plants in a sunny spot, you can bring them in for the winter months until spring.

If your plants are not yet ready for their final move indoors, they will continue to grow and flourish outdoors in the cold frame or greenhouse until they are ready.

CUTTINGS

A cut stem can be used to take a new plant.

If you have healthy plant stalks that are at least a foot long, it is best to use them for cuttings because the chances of the new plant being healthy are much better.

1. When you bring your cuttings indoors so that they can begin to grow, make sure they are in a warm, sunny location. The warmer and brighter the weather, the faster they will grow and produce new plants.

2. In about 3–4 weeks, you should see signs of growth.

3. After about 5–6 weeks, your plants should begin to flower and form new seed pods.

4. Once your plants are growing vigorously, it is best to bring them inside so that they can be protected from any late-season frosts or a very early heatwave in the spring.

5. If you have a greenhouse, you can use this as your ideal location.

When your tea plants are ready to be moved indoors, they will have outgrown the cold frame that you used during their early months.

It is best to use a greenhouse in the later months of their growth because it will protect them from any frosts that occur during the spring or fall.

It is best if you place your plants in a sunny location. The temperature will be more regulated as well.

As you continue to grow your tea plants indoors, they will flower and form new seedpods, just like they did when they were growing outside.

HOW TO CHOOSE THE RIGHT CROPS FOR YOUR SOIL AND CLIMATE, STARTING WITH THE TEA PLANT (CAMELLIA) AND GOING ON THROUGH A SURVEY OF TISANES (AKA HERBAL TEAS)

Investing in a small plot of land, or even just a pot on the porch can be rewarding for body and mind. But before you can plant your tea garden, you'll need to know which plants are best to grow in your soil and climate.

If you live in a climate where you have a few months of warm weather and plenty of rain, consider growing camellia sinensis, the tea plant. Tea is an ideal spring plant because it takes a while to mature and, even once it does produce leaves; it is not harvested until later in the season. This makes it suitable for many home gardeners. If you just want to start a small garden and don't have enough space, consider growing the camellia sinensis var. assamica, the tea plant; this variety is hardier and will survive in much colder climates. Growing tisanes can be very rewarding, but there are many choices to make about what you can grow in your garden.

How to Choose the Right Crops For Your Soil and Climate, Going on Through a Survey of Tisanes (Aka Herbal Teas)

Tisanes are herbs, plants, and sometimes trees that are used to make herbal teas. They are teas made from any plant or tree other than the tea plant, camellia sinensis. Tisanes can be made from any number of plants, including fruit and vegetables, but the most popular herbs for making tea are mints, rose hips, chamomile, and citrus trees.

In addition to tea, herbal teas contain other medicinal properties. Originally, the best quality herbal teas had a reputation for healing the heart and blood vessels, but these days some people use them instead of prescription medicines. Today, tisanes are more often used to treat insomnia or add flavor to cooking than they are for medical purposes.

The value of herbs like mint and chamomile in tea is controversial. People either love them or hate them, depending on their tastes. Others, like me, find that their stomach is sensitive to tisanes made from peppermint or chamomile. Many other herbs can be used to make tea, and the best way to discover which ones you like most is to experiment.

Luckily, if you are interested in adding herbs to your garden, many of them are easy to grow. Mints and rose hips will spread themselves without much help from you, but chamomile will need some love or it will wither away.

Herbal tea can be grown in the shade of trees and shrubs, but only in the shade. The most important part of growing herbs is to provide excellent drainage because with excess moisture they will rot quickly. Placing

your herb garden where you won't see it much or trim it often is a good idea.

If you have a small garden and want to grow something that will grow well there, try growing a perennial for your tea: rose hips, camellia sinensis var. assamica, citrus trees, or citrus hybrids. If you want an herb that doesn't mind a shady spot and won't spread much if you don't keep it trimmed, try growing mints. You could use an indoor container for mints: a large ball of potting soil in a pot on the porch would work well. With most herbs, keep them well watered and they'll thrive.

Chapter - 7
HOW TO CHOOSE THE RIGHT CROPS FOR YOUR SOIL AND CLIMATE?

There are many factors that you need to take into consideration when starting a tea garden, but the first one is really to think about what crops are best suited to your soil and climate. There are 2 kinds of plants that grow well in most climates: evergreen trees like ilex or magnolia, which will require little maintenance aside from pruning; and plants like lavender or avocados, which will require more attention than other crops. Evergreen plants can become quite large and require quite a bit of space, so, in your first garden, you may want to focus on evergreen trees. Lavender crops are often grown as annuals, so they will only need to be replaced every 2 years. Avocados may be grown for their leaves or the fruit inside them. The leaves are used in a lot of tea blends for their flavor and the seeds can be pressed to make avocado oil. You will be able to harvest the fruit in late fall. Many evergreen trees are also medicinal or have some other use. For example, ilex is used as an ingredient in toothpaste and as a tea for digestive issues. Magnolia leaves are useful in the treatment of asthma. Within your tea garden, you should have a few different trees that serve different purposes:

The 2 best choices for your first garden will be evergreen trees with edible or medicinal leaves.

To get your tea garden started, you will need to purchase some trees or start seeds indoors. You can buy ilex from online nurseries, but if you want something unique to your area, then it may be a better idea to start with seeds or bare-root plants. Many people grow their cane from seed or from canes they purchased from a nursery, though I would not recommend doing this for your first garden. First off, trees can take anywhere from three to eight years to mature (sometimes even longer), and by that time they are quite large. In addition, you will have to prune and shape them every year and often trim the branches to be able to see the leaves clearly.

After purchasing your tree or starting it indoors, ilex roots do not transplant well. For this reason, it may be a better idea to plant them in your garden as opposed to trying to move them. It is also a good idea to plant trees that are already mature at the same time as you are planting another tree so that you can compare their

growth rate. Ilex should be planted about three feet apart and should be allowed to grow freely without any trimming for their first year. In the second year, you will need to prune out most of the branches to expose the leaves and prevent disease.

Ilex will grow to be quite large and require a lot of space.

If you purchase bare-root plants, then you will need to plant them in your garden after the ground has warmed up. Bare root plants take time to start growing and will only produce foliage after a few weeks, but they do not have the same size restrictions as trees. If you do not want to buy a tree or start one from seed, then you can also purchase varieties of ilex that are grown specifically for their tea leaves.

The sunny aspect of your garden will allow for more leaf growth.

Once you have your tea garden planted and growing, you should now start to think about what crops to grow inside it. For example, lemongrass is a very common ingredient in many blends. Being a tropical plant, lemongrass will need to be grown outdoors to produce usable leaves; however, if you live in an area that has a lot of cold winters (like northern New England), then you may have to consider indoor plantations instead. Lemon verbena may also be grown indoors, but it will require a lot of light to produce the best quality leaves.

Cinnamon is another crop that will thrive in a sunny garden. It grows well inside and can be hung up from the ceiling or clipped to make it look better. For a small garden, dried cinnamon sticks can be readily purchased at many supermarkets and grocery stores. Cinnamon sticks also work well in teas, but they may be too strong for some people.

Cloves are an autumn crop that is useful both in blends and as a spice. They grow best from seeds, so it is best to wait until your spring planting season to plant them. They can be grown indoors in a pot or outside in a sun-drenched area.

Another crop that works well with lemongrass is peppermint. This will help repel pests like bees and wasps from your garden. Peppermint can be bought in a variety of forms: seed, root, or herb. It grows best in full sunlight but can also be grown indoors.

If you have a sunny garden with an abundance of space, then bergamot is the crop for you. Bergamot is often used to make Earl Grey tea and can be grown from seeds or a cutting. The best method to plant bergamot is from a cutting and will require two years before it flowers.

In summary, you will need to be very careful to grow the right crops inside your ilex tea garden. For example, mint should only be grown if it is the correct variety, and ginger should only be grown if you are using a greenhouse. Each crop has its benefits and drawbacks, so with a bit of effort, you can grow some great teas for your friends or family!

Chapter - 8
HOW TO GROW A LARGE VARIETY OF PLANTS IN YOUR GARDEN, ON A BALCONY, OR EVEN ON A WINDOW

Imagine being able to experience a huge variety of flavors with just 1 cup of tea. Growing your garden can be a great way to enhance the quality and flavor of your tea for much less than you would pay at the store, as well as providing beautiful flowers in the spring and summer months.

You don't need a lot of space for this project—it's possible on even the smallest of balconies or windowsills. These are the basic steps needed to get started.

First, find a sunny location that receives 6–8 hours of sunlight per day. Choose a spot with good drainage and be sure that it gets enough rain to stay moist, but not so much that it's constantly wet.

Next, come up with a design for your garden. A simple design is usually best as you can grow smaller plants in small pots or even inside the planters themselves. Choose plants that will grow well in your climate and pay attention to the care requirements for each plant or seed you are interested in growing.

Finally, it's time to start planting! You might like to start with a few tomato plants, which are easy to grow and produce delicious red fruits. Once you see how easy it is to grow tomatoes your choices will be endless. Choose a variety that will grow well in your climate and pay attention to the care requirements for each plant or seed you are interested in growing.

For a successful garden, choose plants that will mature at roughly the same time so there won't be too many ripening all at once.

A word of caution when watering. Do not allow your plants to sit in water, this will cause them to rot and die. Check the soil daily, to see if it needs watering. If the top 1–2-inch of soil feels dry, it's time to water.

You might be tempted to plant a variety of herbs, but it's much more fun (and nutritious) to have a mixture of tea-related and other plants. A few ideas for tea-related plants are chamomile, elderberry, lime tree, lavender, and peppermint.

I suggest growing lots of different varieties of mint, but not too many because each variety requires a different growing season so you can't just start minting whenever things get dry. If you grow enough, you can experiment with different varieties. On sunny days the mint will grow rapidly, but if it's raining it will slow down and produce more leaves.

It's important to pick places for your plants that are sheltered from the wind and full sun, such as behind a wall or fence, next to your back door, or under an overhang. Once you have stuck your plants in, be sure to keep an eye on watering. The soil should feel dry a few inches down but you should add more water every few days if the leaves are very dry. Often people write to me saying their mint is dying. Don't panic and try to water it when it's not too hot because the roots need some air to breathe and it will just cause the mint to rot, even though the leaves are still green.

In my garden, I have a small shelf that is level with the surface of my balcony which I usually add more plants to as they die. If you get a cute little cactus (I got mine for free at the local garden center) it will also make a good perch for your bird or cat.

Once your plants are established, you can use them for lots of different kinds of tea and to flavor foods. The oils in tea plants are much stronger than those in herbs, so you only need a small number of tea leaves to flavor a dish. For example, to make minted peas, you just need a few sprigs of mint and peas.

I have made very tasty peppermint carrots by cutting carrots into short lengths and poking three or four branches of peppermint into each one, propping them up with skewers until the carrot tops grew over the mint and then just leaving them until the carrots were soft enough to eat. I have also made delicious summer squash by cutting two pumpkins into half-moons and sticking these in a vase to catch the honey I was making and then adding more pumpkins and honey until the squashes were big enough. I have made gorgeous fudge by melting sugar with peppermint tea syrup, stirring it all together really quickly so that the mint didn't get to taste too strongly of sugar, dipping fruit into melted candy, and then baking it for a few minutes. I made a delicious spiced pear from pears which I soaked in the tea for a few days, and then added some sugar and a little water to make syrup. I even made my brandy by soaking raisins in coffee, then pouring the coffee into strong espresso. You can also use mint to make jellies, ice cream, and teas for cooking, and so on.

Chapter - 9
HOW TO GROW AND CARE FOR YOUR PLANTS

Tea is the second most popular drink in the world, after water. It has been shown to help lower blood pressure, increase your metabolic rate, and help you burn fat more effectively.

Growing your own tea garden can be an incredibly rewarding experience that will not only provide you with fresh and healthy tea leaves that are truly organic but it'll also provide a tranquil escape from the hustle and bustle of everyday life.

PICKING THE LOCATION

Choose a site that is away from the direct sunlight and one which has full access to water. If possible it should also be sheltered from any strong winds or cold winds. The soil should be fertile and damp but if you notice any dry patches try applying some additional water. If you feel that there is any chance of your tea plants being near dogs, cats, or other pets then don't plant them in your garden as they will take a liking to them.

PREPARING THE GROUND

Your tea plants will need a lot of water so prepare the ground by digging down and turning over the soil. Also, dig out any weeds that may be present. If there is a lot of extra dirt then you'll need to remove it or your tea plants won't receive the right amount of drainage. If your tea plants are very young they could be susceptible to frost so if there is any chance of this happening protect them by covering them with hay, straw, or other material to protect them from the cold.

PLANTING YOUR PLANTS

1. Place your tea plants into small containers/pots filled with potting soil and water them. Make sure to check that there are no green or yellow leaves. If you're not sure then dip your finger into the soil and if it's moist and healthy then your plants are ready for planting out in the garden.

2. Plant them evenly around each other but do not cover the roots as much of their growth will be stunted which will develop poorly shaped leaves.

3. Ensure that there is at least a 2 ft. distance between your tea plants and any other nearby plants or hedges. This will allow your tea to develop unhindered fully.

4. Water them again to make sure that they are moist and then cover them with a thick layer of mulch, straw, leaves, or even grass clippings to protect the roots and keep the soil moist.

5. Water them again every couple of days or when the top few inches of soil dry up.

6. Finally, budget for an afternoon pass time and plan to spend some quality alone or with friends bonding with nature as you watch your tea plants grow.

PEST AND DISEASES CONTROL

A tea garden can provide an enjoyable hobby for beginners and advanced gardeners alike. Unfortunately, many factors can affect the success of your garden. Among these is pest and disease control, which you should take into consideration when planting new plants or continuing to nurture existing plants. Read on for more information about the types of pests that could be harmful to your tea gardens along with their signs, prevention tips, and natural pest management strategies.

Scale insects are among the world's most destructive pests that can become a problem in your garden if steps are not taken to control them. These sap-sucking insects tend to attack plants of all sizes and are extremely hardy. They also move quickly, making them hard to find, and their waxy bodies make it more difficult for chemicals to stick. The damage done by scale is easily identified by yellowish-brown, tar spots on the leaves of your plants. A lot of damage can be done to your plants by scale, as they suck the sap from the plant. In some cases these pests can transmit viruses from one plant to another, so be sure to seek out a natural treatment for these pests as soon as possible.

Spider mites are another common problem in many tea gardens. These tiny arachnids feed on the underside of leaves, causing them to become yellow or silver. Other symptoms include brown spots on the leaves and new plant growth stunted. These can be easily identified by the presence of webbing on leaves. Spider mites can reproduce quickly and are hard to control with chemical pesticides, so seek out a natural solution to these pests before they take over your garden like they do in certain parts of the world.

Fungus gnats are small flying insects that develop hitchhiking fungus spores around plants or other objects, including your garden's soil. Other symptoms include plants that are stunted or leaves that have a pale appearance. You can identify these pests by observing their small size, movement, and presence around your plants. The best thing to do is to avoid growing any plant that the pest is prevalent in as it will only lead to more serious problems for your garden.

Multiple types of herbivores can be a threat to your garden, including slugs, snails, aphids, and caterpillars. Each one of these can be a threat to your garden, but one of the most common is the slug. These are among the tiniest field-side pests, and they feed on all types of garden plants. While other pests feed on leaves, these slugs eat roots. If they manage to eat more than just your roots, damage will occur in your plants' stems and branches. You can recognize the presence of slugs by their small size and their characteristic trails behind them as they move around a lawn or garden.

If you live in an area where these pests are a problem, be sure to take steps to reduce their numbers in your garden. These can be destructive even in small quantities, so do your research and take the necessary steps to protect your garden and plants from harm.

Tea plants are subject to a variety of pests. Pest management can be done with different methods and

materials, including chemical pesticides, cultural controls, and natural controls.

Pesticides can be used as an alternative method to control pests, especially if you are not able or comfortable doing other types of pest control. With proper use, pesticides will kill a wide range of insect pests that could negatively affect your tea gardens. Some species of insects, however, may still exist even after the use of certain pesticides. This is attributed to the "re-emergence" of the insect in question, which means that even though it was killed off by the pesticide it continues to survive on a different part of the plant. One way to prevent this is by using other control methods, such as cultural control. Maintaining healthy plants will help a lot in keeping pests at bay.

Pest management with pesticides should always be followed by proper quarantine. Quarantine refers to preventing the spread of the pests themselves. Pests such as insects and mites are often mobile organisms, and depending on the type of materials that you use for pest control, these pests could continue to exist even after treated. As a part of quarantine, any plants or materials that were exposed to pesticides should not be used for 1–2 years after treatment.

Cultural controls are methods to keep pests under control. They include plant and insect predators, and diseases. Preventative measures against pests include regular inspections for pest signs, checking the plants for damage, removing infected plants as soon as possible with good soil management practices, planting hardier tea types that are less susceptible to pests, and selecting crop areas based on a variety of factors (weather, soil conditions).

When using cultural controls, it is important to know the rules for each type of control.

Spot treatments are a form of cultural control. The spot treatment uses biological organisms that are naturally present on plants, usually microorganisms. These organisms will feed on pest insects, and the result is an attack on both pests and beneficial insects. These systems can be used with potentially dangerous pathogens, such as pest-eating nematodes or insect parasitoids.

Biological controls are a form of organic pest control or integrated pest management. In this method, species that exhibit antagonistic or parasitic behavior towards the target pests are released into the environment. The natural enemies of a specific pest can be identified and introduced to diminish the population size, or even eradicate it. Examples are the wasps used against caterpillars, fishes, and cats to control aphids and mites, ladybugs for their herbivore on aphids and scale insects, and spiders for their predation on insect pests.

Herbivorous insects are used by gardeners to control pests. As predators, herbivorous insects feed on a wide range of pests for example; ladybugs eat aphids, lacewing larvae, and aphid eggs, and nymphs as well as other insect larvae at hatching. Aphid parasitoids are also an effective form of pest management which will lay their eggs onto the surface of the pest aphids or mites which they take over and parasitize.

The sticky traps method is usually a temporary solution for pest control and will not be effective on it. If

done at the early stages of infestation, it can be an easy way to reduce crop damage. Sticky traps are used as a monitoring system where they are hung on the plant and used to monitor pests so that timely control operations can be done when necessary. The materials commonly used for these traps are different types of adhesives.

Other methods of pest prevention include the use of natural predators, which can be achieved through biological and cultural means. Natural predators can also help control the population size of pests. These include entomopathogenic nematodes, mites, and insects that parasitize on other insects.

The practice of integrated pest management is a tool used to reduce the use of pesticides in commercial crop production. Integrated pest management is a more environmentally friendly method that allows for the use of pesticides in certain situations, such as when the pests are not under control or when other techniques have failed. Integrated pest management includes the use of biological controls and the use of non-chemical tools.

Natural controls are methods of preventing pest outbreaks. Good drainage of soil is essential for keeping roots free from blockages, which could predispose plants to diseases. Good soil moisture management and avoiding over-watering are also necessary, as this can lead to increased pest populations. If fertilizers are used, they should be of good quality and not contain too much nitrogen. Planting resistant plant varieties is a good choice, as plants that can tolerate pests in high concentrations will outgrow pests that are not affected by high pest populations. Organic matter is a good supplement to regular soil. Soil should be allowed to rest from time to time and heavily infested areas should be replanted, as it is much easier to control pests at the onset of their outbreak.

If your tea plants become overwhelmed with pests, you may need to use stronger pesticides and other methods of controlling them. Getting rid of pests early on can save you a lot of money in lost crops later on.

Chapter - 10
INSTRUCTIONS FOR GROWING TEA IN CONTAINER GARDENS AND RAISED BEDS

The art and science of growing tea are quite simple. The complexity comes in with the various types of teas that can be grown. The process for growing and making tea is along the same lines as growing any other plant in your garden or container planter. The goal is to have plants that will provide you with a long harvest of good-tasting and health-promoting herbal tea.

Growing tea in container gardens and raised beds can be extremely rewarding as you can maintain lush, healthy growth in your garden year after year.

The two most important factors to consider when growing tea are: the growing area (container or bed) and the variety of tea to be grown.

The growing area, whether it is in a container garden or a bed, should be about 5 square feet (1 square foot = 9-inch diameter) less than the size of the average pot you will use for planting your seeds.

For example, if you plan to plant 6-inch pots in your garden, then you should grow plants that will fit into 5-inch pots.

For best results, use small or miniature pot sizes for growing tea. In a word, don't plant tea in 10-inch pots.

The variety of tea to be grown can come down to personal preference. Some varieties are much easier to grow than others.

There are many different types of teas that one can grow in a container garden or bed, each with its advantages and disadvantages. The following are some of the most common teas that can be grown in a container.

White and green teas are both made from the leaves of the Camellia sinensis plant. White is typically steamed to create a light, soft tea while green tea is typically made by fermenting the leaves to produce a robust, bold-tasting tea. Both teas come in different varieties, each with its distinct flavor and color. Green

tea is typically grown in the sun while White tea is usually grown under shade.

White, green, or oolong tea can be grown in a container garden year-round. (It does well in warm summer months when temperatures are above 75 °F.

Never let your container plants dry out. Water your plants regularly and deeply so they have enough time to absorb the water and develop strong root systems. There are many different types of tea plants and each is best grown in certain climates and situations.

Camellia sinensis can be grown in containers year-round. The plant is very hardy with few problems, but it does require a little extra care during cold winter months because it does not tolerate freezing temperatures well.

Vermont mountain tea (camellia assamica) is one of the most common varieties of tea used to make various herbal teas. It is a vigorous grower that only needs full sun. It is also capable of surviving in cool, damp areas but grows best in areas with just enough soil moisture to make tea leaves fully expand and develop their maximum flavor.

This long leaf plant grows well with containers, but it does need ample room to grow. This plant will tolerate a wide range of temperatures and does well in warm and cool weather alike. It requires a lot of water and soil to thrive.

This tall, leggy plant can grow up to 20 ft. and is moderately hardy in the North but will require extra care in colder climates and places that get severe winters. It will also do better in warmer areas with regular watering. Camellia sasanqua produces a light, highly aromatic tea that is green in color but has a distinct floral taste.

This tea plant produces a light tea that is white and has a milder taste than green or black tea. It is best grown in the sun and should be watered regularly.

A very hardy, compact bush with bright green leaves and a pleasant flavor. The plants are resistant to most diseases and do well in all climate zones. They require little care and grow very quickly although they will take up to 4 years before producing full-size leaves.

This is another highly productive plant that has high disease resistance and only needs good amounts of sunlight. It will take up to 3 years to produce full-size leaves.

A small, compact bush with glossy green leaves that are tightly rolled. It does well in sunny or partly shaded areas and produces small but fragrant tea leaves with a mild flavor.

Another popular variety that grows into a small bush with long, slender leaves and a strong flavor. It is easy to grow with high resistance to many common diseases.

For all tea plants, it would be advantageous to add in a little compost or fertilizer after plants have started

sprouting, but before they go into the ground.

When planting your seeds or seedlings, you will want to consider the following:

Plant tea bushes at least 2 ft. apart from the center of the plant to the center of the plant if you are planting in a raised bed and about 1 ft. apart if you are planting in containers. For container gardens, allow plants to grow about 2-inch during the first year to develop their root systems fully. Planting the taller varieties of plants will require a little more space than planting shorter varieties.

Plant tea seeds in moist potting mix or soil as soon as possible after you get them home. Place the seeds in a cool place where they can be kept below 78 °F until they germinate.

Place your plants in a well-lit area with plenty of sunlight. If possible, it would be best to set them out in the spring so that they can get used to the warmth and the direct sunlight before winter.

Fresh Mountain or desert tea (camellia sinensis var. assamica) can be planted outdoors in regular garden soil 4–6 weeks after the last spring frost.

Growers can grow tea in various types of containers filled with potting mix, not just outdoor gardens. Tea plants tend to grow quickly and get large, so it is best to use larger containers. Watering your tea plants should be done regularly as they are very thirsty and have shallow roots.

Plant the tea seeds about ½-inch deep in the soil and then water them well with room temperature water. Do not use warm or cold water, as this will kill your seeds.

If you are growing tea from seeds, be sure that they are fresh and not dried out.

Your plants must get plenty of sunlight so be sure to give them adequate sunlight in a well-ventilated area. As with all plants, tea plants need lots of water during their first year.

Chapter - 11
HELPFUL DEVELOPMENT COUNSEL OF THE PLANTS

Tea is a favorite and the most famous beverage in the world, second only to water. If you would like to grow your own tea garden and have it as an attractive part of your garden, you need to know which plants are tea, especially the things you need to consider about selecting and arranging it.

It is very easy to propagate and maintain tea plants. Tea bushes grow quite tall, but many people do not have enough space for them in their garden. It is usually grown in a container because it is less expensive. These plants can also be grown in containers on the patio or even inside your house with sufficient sunlight and fresh air.

You can start with a small plant that will grow into a tree-like bush that can eventually grow to a height of three feet. If you want older plants, it would be best to look for them in specialty nurseries or online since they can be sold at a very low price.

If you choose the smaller one, then place it in a sunny spot with a moderate amount of water. As the plant grows, make sure to prune it and keep it healthy. You can also water again to help it grow faster.

When it reaches about 2 ft., you can choose to plant it in a larger pot. Make sure also to fertilize the soil. You will see more blossoms after a month if you have been giving proper care and nourishment to the plants.

To have your tea garden, make sure that you select the right plant for planting and follow the guidelines on how to maintain it properly.

However, it is best to allow its natural growth for it to produce leaves that are high in quality and of excellent flavor.

Before planting, it is best to determine the best place to plant the tea garden. This should be a little bit away from other plants and trees so that the tea can have enough sunlight to grow. It is also important to

remember that it needs a lot of water during the first few months of transplanting so that you will be able to grow healthy and strong plants. Also, make sure that you plan on maintaining and caring for your plants regularly so that they can flourish.

Once the plant has grown, it needs to be pruned and shaped to fit the container. Most of the time, it will need topiary care and attention to avoid it from growing too wide that your pot cannot fit anymore.

The best way to garden with tea is by planting seeds in a pot once you have grown your plants. In this case, you only need a handful of seeds.

Take the actual seeds and put them in the soil. You can also mix them along with the soil so that they can grow successfully.

Once you have done this, place it in a sunny spot where you will see the new plants sprout.

It is best to keep them watered a couple of times a week to make sure that they are growing well. The most important thing is that you prepare a good environment for your tea plants for them to thrive and grow well.

Before you plant your tea plants, make sure to know which tea is best for you. There are several varieties of tea in the world. Each type has a different flavor and purpose in your life.

For example, Green tea is very useful for daily health and also tastes good as infused teas and drinks. You can find so many different types of green teas including black, white, and oolong all of which have different features.

There are various ways to garden with tea. Some people prefer to grow their own plants while others prefer growing little sprouts inside the soil. It is all up to you on how you want to manage the growth of your plants for your tea garden.

You may find that growing your tea garden is quite easy once you have done it over time. It can be a very delightful activity if you know what you are doing.

If you want to have a healthy drink, you will need to add some fresh ingredients to your tea. You can use fresh milk, honey, or sugar for your tea. Alternatively, you can also prepare some great hot teas by adding other ingredients to it like coffee or cocoa powder.

If you are thinking about growing your plants, make sure that you are taking care of them well. Also, keep them watered and groomed regularly so that they won't wilt and lose their stamina.

There are also some tips that you can try to have a great-looking and healthy tea garden. For example, you can add different herbs to the soil so that it will help improve the overall growth rate of the plant. A basil plant is known to provide extra health benefits for your plants and flowers.

There are many other options like planting different flowers and various plants so that your garden will look alive and attractive.

You can also include some colorful plants on the ground so that it will give a little bit of color to how your tea garden looks.

You must clean your garden regularly for it to remain healthy and clean. Also, do not forget to add fertilizer if you are planning on growing your plants for a while. Make sure that the fertilizer is organic and has been mixed with organic substances so that you can have healthy plants which will produce great tasting tea for life.

If you want to keep your tea garden clean and beautiful, it is advisable to plant some industrial-grade plants in your garden. There are lots of varieties available which will grow quickly and provide a lot of strength for the plants. Alternatively, you can also place the plants in pots so that they will take up less space on your patio without affecting its beauty and appearance.

Chapter - 12
HARVESTING

If you're thinking of growing more than one tea plant, harvest the leaves from lower on the plant first, as these will have matured.

Harvesting will take place four times a year: in late summer and early autumn after the new leaves have grown; in late autumn and early winter before frost has killed all foliage; in spring just before new growth appears, and between cuts when teas are being made.

No matter your timetable for harvesting, harvest only mature leaves that are fully opened. You'll be able to see if the leaf is fully opened when you hold it up to a light source. Look for a clear light patch, without any white edges.

Pick leaves progressively from the tea plant, leaving at least three leaves on each branch to help support the plant as it grows.

Once you've finished harvesting, gather dried leaves into bundles that are small enough to fit into your cooking pot easily and tie them with string.

WHICH PARTS OF THE PLANT ARE USED TO MAKE TEA

Tea is a drink that's been around for centuries. The tradition of drinking tea goes back as far as the 5th century in China, and it has since spread throughout the world and become a staple of life.

As with any other dish, there are many different types of tea to try. Particular parts of the plant are used to make tea, depending on where it is being prepared. If you want to make good tea, you should be able to identify the parts of the plant by their different names.

Tea leaves are used for making tea leaves. These are popularly known as "tea plants". Tea plants can be divided into two categories: single shoots and bushes. The leaves that are made from single shoots are slightly

darker in color compared to those made from bushes.

- **Leaf:** This is the youngest part of the plant. It has a small amount of chlorophyll in it. These are mostly used in cooking, which is why leafy vegetables are black in color.

- **Stem, stem tea:** The stem of the plant is an elongated and stiffened part. It bears buds like leaves and can produce additional stems through these buds. Like leaves, stalks are also edible. The main ingredient in most tea bags is the stem.

- **Shoot, shoot tea:** Shoots are the newest parts of the plant. They are edible and can be prepared as you would with any other type of vegetable. However, they tend to be slightly bitter in flavor. Shoots are generally fried before they are served as a side dish or an appetizer.

- **Leaf bud, leaf bud tea:** The leaf bud is the point where all leaves converge on and grow from. It is the part of the plant that bears tiny, white flowers that develop into fruits.

- **Flower, flower tea:** This is the flowering part of the plant. These are quite different from the leaf buds in terms of their appearance and taste. Flowers tend to be slightly sour, but they are also more aromatic than any other part of the plant.

- **Young shoot, young shoot tea:** The young shoot is a stressed phrase for leaf shoots. It is the newest

part of the plant.

- **Root, root tea:** The roots are the part of the plant that holds it to the ground. The roots of some plants have been known to kill off other plants before they can even grow up to become a mature part of their plant. However, this is not the case for all of them.

- **Root tea tips:** The stems of most plants have been known to contain chemicals that help in killing pathogens or microbes that can cause diseases like diarrhea and worms.

- **Marrow, bone tea:** Marrow is the inner part of the stem. Its shape is that of a bone. It can be consumed as an ingredient in certain dishes or used to add flavor to soups and stews.

- **Wood, wood tea:** This is the outer part of the plant used for making furniture or building houses. These are often referred to as trees because they can grow to a size that's much larger than other parts of plants. These can be sold by the ton. There are different types of wood that contain varying levels of aromatic and non-aromatic properties.

- **Fruit, fruit tea:** The fruit is a special type of bud. It refers to the colorless or brownish capsule that contains a few tiny seeds within it. Fruits are very flavorful and can be used in baking such as muffins or cakes.

- **Seed, seed tea:** The seed is the last part of the plant that you will find. Seeds are produced by the fruit and are used to plant new plants. Seeds are usually preserved in olive oil or vinegar to improve their shelf life. They can also be ground and prepared as tea.

Different parts of the plant are used to make different types of tea. The leaves are usually steeped, and the buds are often dried and then steeped in hot water. Sometimes other parts of the plant, like stems and roots, can be used as well. In some cases, the leaves are roasted before they are steeped.

WHAT MAKES OOLONG TEA OOLONG?

Oolong tea, sometimes called "the wine of tea" or "half-fermented tea", is partially fermented. It is made from leaves that have been allowed to dry out and turn yellowish before the oxidation process begins. Depending on the length of the oxidation period, the resulting tea can range from greenish-yellow to brownish-red in color.

WHAT MAKES BLACK TEA BLACK?

Black tea is fully fermented and is made from fully dried leaves. During the fermentation process, this lasts several hours, enzymes break down the leaves' chlorophyll. This gives the tea the yellowish-red to a brown color characteristic of most teas. These days, black teas have become synonymous with malty Assam blends

or robust Indian Darjeelings, which are sometimes blended with flavored teas to create a more balanced product.

WHAT MAKES PU-ERH TEA PU-ERH?

Pu-erh is a very special tea, unique among teas in that it is fermented for several years before it is produced. It can be aged for decades or even centuries. The name "Pu-erh" comes from the Chinese pronunciation of the word "pu'er." During the fermentation process, spores (the living cells of fungi) are added to the tea leaves to speed up the aging process.

HOW IS TEA BREWED?

Many different methods can be used to brew tea. Traditional English tea makes use of the water boiled with the leaves, while French press brewing involves squeezing out the leaves and then adding cold water directly into a cup. One of the most popular methods of making tea is using an electric kettle. The leaf is placed in a basket, which fits over a kettle base. It then comes to a boil, permitting steam to collect in the basket during steeping. These kettles let you use smaller tea amounts by measuring the right amount of water and leaf.

WHAT IS SHENG (ALSO CALLED RAW) TEA?

Sheng is the unfermented tea leaf, from which all other varieties of tea are derived. Because this fresh leaf contains more delicate flavors than the other varieties of tea, it is prized by many for its ability to enhance a dish without overpowering it. It is often used in combination with the more well-known flavors of Pu-erh and black teas.

WHAT IS GREEN TEA?

Green tea is a type of unfermented tea made from the leaves of the Camellia sinensis plant. These leaves are first steamed, then dried, and rolled into small balls. The drying process creates a tint to the leaf which makes it darker than other varieties of tea, creating a lighter-colored cup of tea when brewed. Green tea is still very popular in Eastern countries such as China, Japan, and Korea due to its health benefits and positive effects on the body's metabolism.

Green tea is made from young tea leaves and is therefore naturally green in color. Because it is made from such young leaves, green tea contains higher levels of chlorophyll than other teas. The chlorophyll reacts with the enzymes that break down the caffeine in your stomach to give you that "grassy" flavor found in most green teas.

WHEN AND HOW TO HARVEST YOUR TEA PLANTS?

Tea plants can be harvested anytime after they reach a height of five to six feet—usually somewhere between three and eight years. It's important to know how long a plant will take to reach this height before harvesting it in order to get the highest quality leaves for making tea, which are most flavorful when picked early. To harvest your tea plants:

1. Cut off the top of the stem with a sharp hand pruner, and then cut down the length of the stem with scissors.

2. When the stem is cut, carefully remove the leaves up to eye level without disturbing or breaking any of the branches. Do not leave any stems lying on the ground, as this will cause new growth to delay in producing leaves, which reduces quality. For larger plants, we recommend leaving at least a few leaves at eye level until the top growth starts to die and becomes more difficult to handle when harvested.

3. To harvest the tea plants, tie a length of string to the side of the plant. Gently pull it down to remove all of the leaves.

4. Collect all of your top growth in one place to use for withering and drying.

5. As soon as possible after harvesting, arrange your top growth in a large box and cover it with cheesecloth or muslin. The warmer climate during late summer slows photosynthesis, giving your leaves a long time to become dry. This is also the time that they will be most fragrant.

6. Wither your leaves in a warm place, such as outside on a breezy day or on top of a water heater, with ample ventilation.

7. Once dry, remove leaves from the cheesecloth and package them in plastic bags or tea balls.

In more temperate climates, such as those found in New England and Japan, green tea can be used when it is harvested as soon as the first leaf appears. In more tropical regions, the tea plants are left to grow larger, and new growth is harvested once a year.

Green tea should be harvested in early spring and summer when the leaves are young and tender. Leaves picked later in the season will be more difficult to wither and dry naturally, as they will contain less moisture. This is one of the downsides of green tea production compared to black tea; it requires more attention because it needs a warm environment with sufficient ventilation to allow for complete drying between harvest times.

Since green tea is harvested at the same time as black tea, it is not necessary to wither and dry the leaves earlier than black tea. When green tea production becomes commercialized, you will see that the leaves are picked at regular intervals throughout the year, but this is a result of concerns for quality rather than cost.

Chapter - 13
HOW TO GATHER, DRY, AND STORE YOUR TEA

Tea, in particular green and black tea, is a worldwide favorite steeped in tradition. Whether you're a novice tea drinker or an avid collector, it's important to know the best ways to care for your plants.

Knowing how to grow and care for your own tea garden is a great way to save some money, get fresh produce from the comfort of your home, and enjoy all the benefits that come with drinking healthy tea.

You can't grow tea in your backyard, but you can make sure your plants are healthy and happy by learning how to harvest, dry/ferment properly, and store your tea.

GATHER

Before you begin, make sure that your container is big enough to accommodate the amount of plant material you plan on harvesting. Once your plants are dry, they will shrink and some may crumble a little. You're not looking for exact measurements so don't worry too much about how full it looks now.

1. Cut as many leaves and stems as you want into pieces that are 3–4-inch long or larger (unless you're using fresh mint).

2. Place all cuttings into the container or bags.

3. Tie up the top of the bag if you're using one and store it in a dry area at room temperature for 1–3 months (the longer, the better).

DRYING

If you're using a dehydrator, start with the obvious: dry your herbs. Place your leaves and stems into the dehydrator and check them periodically, allowing extra time for drying if they are rotted or moldy.

For space-saving, you can also choose to dry your herbs in the oven at a lower temperature (200 °F) or place them in an old-fashioned bread machine. Though you cannot adjust the time or temperature on a bread machine, you can start out with herbs and slowly add in more as it gets closer to dry.

The best way to tell if your herbs are dry is to break one of the stems. If there is a snap (or ka-pow) sound, then they are ready. You can also use the stem test for plants like mint and sage where you do not necessarily want the leaves to be completely dried.

Remember, if your herbs are dusty, or not crunchy enough, then you will want to spread them out some more and let them dry for a while.

STORING

Once your herbs are dried you can store them in an airtight container or bag. Hopefully, you have some extra storage space because it's time to start sucking up tea!

1. Place your herbs in the container or bag.

2. Tie up the top of the bag if you're using one and store it in a dry area at room temperature for one to three months (the longer, the better).

3. Once ready, open your container or bag and drink all that you want!

4. Reuse tea bags to store new herbs from other plants that you have grown.

5. If you have fresh mint, separate it from your other plants and keep it in water (like a bouquet) so it doesn't dry out.

STEP-BY-STEP INSTRUCTIONS FOR PLUCKING, WITHERING

The most common method is to strip the leaves of their stems and wither them. There are two ways of doing this: tarring or panning. Tarring is a simpler process, but it's only practiced in Myanmar and Yunnan Province in China since it doesn't produce as high-quality of a leaf; panning requires more work but provides better results.

1. The first step is to open up the leaves and remove the stalks. It's important that you start with a fresh leaf so that the leaf won't have any bitterness.

2. Depending on how many leaves you're going to be harvesting, you need either a small box or a bucket in which to cover them overnight to wither for 3–5 days. Overnight is essential for getting as much moisture out of the leaf as possible because dry tea is not good tea. It should be dark, humid, and quiet during this time.

3. Every day you'll come back to the box or bucket and give it a good shake to bruise the leaves so their juices will come out and fall into a container below.

4. On the third day, you'll notice that the leaves have lost 90% of their weight from water loss.

5. On the 5th day, the leaves are completely dry and ready to be stored or used as they are; this is called "arh te."

There are many methods for plucking, withering, and processing tea. The one described here is the most common way of cultivating and producing white tea.

One method is to pick the buds from the branches of early spring or young plantation tea plants which have not yet produced new shoots. These are laid out to wither on tables. There are several levels of withering: light, medium, or heavy. Light withering means that the tea leaves are dried in bamboo baskets under a layer of straw mats, and medium means that the leaves are dried in wooden trays with a layer of cloth or

paper, while heavy withering means the leaves are plucked dry from the branches. The degree of moisture removal changes depending on the type of tea being made. For white tea, which is produced using buds and very young shoots (new growth), light to medium withering is used when producing green teas and heavy withering when producing black teas. Different withering methods produce different colors and aromas.

Another method is to gather the leaves from whole plantations or tea gardens, which is how most black teas are processed. Because the leaves are not picked from just one branch—as they are during plucking in the case of white tea—the quality of black teas can be lower, although this varies depending on the particular blend.

The next step is to oxidize and dry to produce black or dark teas according to local customs. Lightly oxidized teas all go through a withering process, where the leaves are spread on a clean, open floor or table under the sun until they turn from green to yellow and then to black. The time needed varies depending on weather conditions. The degree of oxidation is determined by drying time. Dark teas such as Oolong and Pu'erh are withered for longer periods.

This is a quick and simple way of making tea. It is favored by those who have very little time or knowledge of processing tea. The leaves are placed in a basket, Oolong stems are added and tied in the basket, which should be made out of copper, plastic, or other non-metal that will not react with the boiling water. The leaves will be picked out after 30–60 minutes depending on the type of tea being made: green teas are often picked at this time.

The tea is boiled, and the leaves are either added to water without boiling or immediately taken out of the kettle. Just before serving, the leaves are removed from the basket and placed in a ceramic pot or bowl. This method is especially popular for Chinese green teas.

Green teas such as "hong cha" and "hong cha bheng" are fermented and kept at an even temperature for a period of "Jia" (3–6 days) until they turn blackish. Then the tea is again boiled before being cooled.

After the leaves have cooled, they are placed in a specific order to steam oxidize for 1–3 hours. The pieces of glass leaves are usually put into a glass bowl and heated on an electric stove, while the pieces of bamboo leaf are boiled in a large iron vat. The leaves can also be placed inside a ceramic pot set over an electric burner. When the tea is ready, it is left alone for an hour to settle before being served or stored until next time.

Chapter - 14
BLENDING TIPS

When you are ready to blend your tea, be sure to use boiling water. You can use a pot, kettle, and "tea ball" or "tea bag" (this is simply a fine mesh fabric that allows passage of water and keeps your tea from being exposed to air) for this purpose. Pour the boiling water over the leaves in your strainer or container with the mesh bag inside and allow it to steep for 3–5 minutes depending on desired strength of the tea. When ready to serve, you can strain the tea into a cup and enjoy it. Or, you can return the tea to your pot and brew it again using boiling water.

When cold-brewing, be absolutely certain that your brewing time is long enough to allow for full extraction of flavor from the leaves. Often people will want to create a lighter or weaker drink when they are using cold-brewing methods. The herb taste varies according to the method used or infused liquid used (e.g. water, alcohol, etc.).

Let us have a look at the top 3 teas that are known for their flavor.

Understand that these are very strong and may not be desirable to those who prefer the milder green teas. You might wish to start with a lesser-quality green tea, which will be much less expensive but will still give you an idea of whether or not you like the taste of green tea.

Green tea is consumed for its many health benefits, and in particular for the lowering of cholesterol. A study published in the "Journal of the American Medical Association" shows that green tea may aid in preventing coronary heart disease and stroke as well as reducing blood pressure. Catechins present in green tea inhibit an enzyme called 4-O-methyl-5-methyltetrahydrofolic acid reductase and thereby prevent its action on NOS (Nitric Oxide Synthase). Nitric oxide is a gas molecule that is beneficial for blood circulation and helps to prevent blood clotting.

While red tea is reported to contain more antioxidants than green, the amount of antioxidants in black tea is significantly higher than in all other teas (more than twice as high as in green tea). Antioxidants are exciting

new players in the field of nutrition. They are best known for helping to fight cancer through their ability to neutralize free radicals. Free radicals have been implicated as one of the causes of some cancers.

There are different types of green tea. The most easily recognizable is the "fermented" kind: this means it's been exposed to bacterial action, and its flavor has been enhanced by the pronounced fermentation. It's also been described as "less bitter than black tea."

One of the best-known varieties is Matcha, which is ground finely and whisked into a pale green paste. The result is a rich, smooth drink that can be used in either hot or cold form. The health benefits of Matcha are similar to those of green tea, and it can be blended with different flavors to create interesting new taste sensations.

Generally speaking, green teas have the lowest caffeine levels and decaffeinated teas have even less. As with wine, lighter-colored teas contain less caffeine than darker teas. Although this is a trend, the differences aren't significant enough for most people to need to worry about them.

There are a wide variety of health benefits that result from drinking tea. Many of these benefits stem from the catechins contained within green tea. Catechins are antioxidants, which means they help protect the body from the ravages of oxidation although it also retains the Epigallocatechin gallate (EGCG) found in green tea. It is this EGCG that appears to benefit health most notably by helping to prevent cancer and heart

disease.

According to a National Cancer Institute study, black tea consumption may reduce the risk of certain cancers. Black tea contains polyphenols—natural chemicals that may prevent cancer-causing substances from being absorbed by your body. The study found that women who drank 3 or more cups of black tea per day had a 20% reduced risk of breast cancer. More research is needed to substantiate these claims, and you should never substitute green tea for black or any other type of tea unless your doctor recommends it for you.

The main health benefits of green tea are attributed to its content of antioxidants, which may help reduce the risk of heart disease. There is also a lot of evidence that supports green tea's effect on lowering bad cholesterol and triglycerides (fat), preventing liver damage, and preventing blood clotting.

BLENDING TEAS AND TISANES

Brewing tea for the perfect cup takes more than boiling water and plopping a teabag in a mug. Tea is an ancient and diverse beverage, with many flavors, aromas, and varieties. Blend your own teas using these steps, or try making tisanes.

Home-brewed teas and tisanes can be used to cure headaches, strengthen immune systems, aid digestion, and more.

Tisanes are made from herbs or flowers in the same way as tea, but tisanes contain simmering water only to release their flavors rather than the full-strength boiling water used for brewing tea. The most common varieties of tisane are mint and chamomile.

MAKING THE PERFECT CUP

Brewing tea can be a complicated process with many steps that vary according to the type of tea being consumed. For the simplest method of brewing, follow these easy steps:

1. Bring water to a boil.

2. Turn off the heat and add loose-leaf tea to water. Steeping times vary widely depending on what type of tea is being brewed, but a good rule of thumb is roughly 1 minute per serving for black teas and white teas and 2 minutes per serving for herbal teas, green teas, or tisanes.

3. Fill your mug with boiling water.

4. Add tea slowly, allowing each cup to steep for a minimum of 1 minute.

5. Strain liquid after steeping by using three layers of cheesecloth or by straining the liquid through a fine-mesh strainer and catching any tea leaves in the sieve.

6. Pour the tea into a tumbler to cool before drinking or use immediately if desired.

BREWING YOUR OWN TEAS

Making your teas and tisanes is a great way to ensure that you are getting the most authentic flavor from your drink. Make sure to follow these steps when blending your own teas:

1. Use fresh produce whenever possible. Botanicals, like Gyokuro, are best when used fresh and unprocessed.

2. Use enough water to immerse the produce; for vegetables, use roughly 6 c. water to 1 c. produce.

3. Allow producing to infuse in the simmering water for at least 20 minutes.

4. Strain the infusion through a fine-mesh strainer lined with cheesecloth or a coffee filter to remove any small bits of plant matter from the tea.

5. Rinse the strainer and cheesecloth thoroughly with cold water to remove any remaining plant matter.

6. Place prepared tea leaves in a muslin bag or tie them into a large muslin cloth and hang upside down on a hook to allow any remaining plant matter to fall into the infuser. Then simply brew as usual.

TASTING TEAS

Once your tea is brewed, try it out before blending your own tisanes by following these guidelines:

1. Steep your tea leaves in hot water for a minimum of 45 seconds.

2. Strain the tea through a fine-mesh strainer to catch any large bits of leaf that may be left on the pan or brewing vessel after steeping.

3. Pour hot water over the leaves and steep again until you get the desired strength of flavor and aroma. Steep as many times as required to achieve a strong flavor, but make sure to stop before too much time is taken out of your brew time.

4. Carefully remove leaves from the tea once blending or steeping is complete to avoid bitterness.

5. Enjoy!

In addition to enjoying the process, drinking tea is a great way to relax and unwind after a long day. Even if you feel like you are tending more to your garden than enjoying it, try steeping some wildflowers today and see how they taste.

HOW TO MAKE UP FRESH AND DRIED TEABAGS AND HOW TO SERVE A DELICIOUS HOMEGROWN TEA

Nowadays, more and more people are looking to live a healthier lifestyle. There are many ways we can try to achieve this, from eating more healthily to indulging in a little home spa treatment. One of the things that contribute to this goal is tea-drinking.

WHY DRINK TEA?

Tea is high in antioxidants, which means that it can help to protect the body against a range of different medical conditions. However, health reasons aside, tea also tastes good and is inexpensive to drink. It's also become increasingly popular with people from all walks of life, thanks to modern packaging methods meaning that making up teabags is a simple and easy task: with just a few ingredients, you can put together homemade teabags for yourself or your family.

What you'll need:

- Fresh tea leaves, or dried if fresh are not available

- Parchment paper

- Matchboxes or empty cardboard tubes (optional)

- Pins or string for making up the teabags (optional)

This is what you do:

1. If you're using dried tea leaves, put them to one side for a moment. Try to choose high-quality tea leaves, as this will make a big difference to the taste of your finished product. If you're using fresh or dried tea leaves, make sure they're either supplied to you in the right kind of packaging or buy them in bulk from a supermarket (or even an online shop).

2. Gather all the ingredients together and put them into a large bowl. You will need to mix water, tea leaves, sugar, and lemon juice.

3. Once mixed thoroughly, pour your mixture through a sieve into 2 separate bowls (one for the dry mixture and one for the wet). Discard the leaves you used to make up the teabag bodies.

4. Mix and put your mixture into matchboxes or empty cardboard tubes (you can use anything that will keep it closed, but don't use plastic). Leave these to one side, covered with a tea towel if you think they're going to be left out for more than 5 minutes.

5. Place your tea bags in the fridge or freezer and wait for a few hours, until they've started to dry out

slightly.

6. Take your teabags out of the fridge or freezer and put them in a bowl. If you're using fresh tea leaves, put them into a bowl and crush them up with a rolling pin (see 1, above). If using dried tealeaves, divide the remaining mixture into 2 bowls: one for the dry mixture and one for the wet. You will then add 1 tbsp. sugar to each bowl 3–5 minutes later.

7. Sprinkle the teabags with the sugar and put them to one side, covered with a tea towel. You can leave them here for as long as you like.

8. Once all your tea bags are made up, you can either put them in a bag or take them to work or school, or if you want them to be ready before dinner time, then they can go into the fridge to wait for a few hours or even overnight.

9. When your teabags are ready, simply pour hot water into a cup and add 1–2 teabags. You'll soon have a delicious cup of homemade tea to enjoy. Remember to keep the unused tea leaves in the fridge or freezer between uses (see 6, above).

When you use up your dried leaves, you can reuse them. Simply put them in a ziplock bag and keep them in the freezer until next time.

Chapter - 15
HOW TO BREW THE PERFECT CUP OF TEA

Tea is one of the most popular beverages in the world, and for good reason. Whether you like your tea hot or cold, black, green, white, or red—there's a type to suit every moment and occasion.

A traditional cup of tea goes beyond just steeped leaves; it's an art form. Steeping time plays an important factor: too long will make a cup bitter while not long enough will result in flat-tasting tea that has no flavor and nobody whatsoever.

Water temperature is another important factor. The hotter the water, the more bitter the tea. For white and green teas, use cooler water around 175 °F. If you are brewing black tea, use boiling water—212 °F should do the trick!

Next, you need to know how long to steep your tea for. Most teas should be steeped for a few minutes, but some can be steeped for as long as five or 10 minutes if you are looking for a unique taste.

Some tea drinkers like to scent their tea by lightly adding a few drops of the herb oils—they're commonly referred to as "tea tannin bags"; others like to add sugar, salt, or lemon for flavor. This is entirely up to you and should be done accordingly depending on your tastes.

After you've steeped your tea leaves, remove them from the heat source and put them in a teapot or other container. Set aside for at least five minutes. Then pour into a mug and garnish with your choice of tea.

The best way to enjoy tea is to have it regularly simply. Having a whole pot of tea you can't get through in one day can lead to the dreaded "black teathole"—that dreaded point where all you want is more, more, more. Once you hit the "teathole," it's a slippery slope to hoarding.

The next time you are craving a hot, steaming cup of tea, make it yourself.

"TEA TOURISM"—VISITING THE SMALL TEA FARMS AROUND THE COUNTRY

The popularity of high-quality tea around the world is leading to a boom in the domestic tea industry. Tea gardens are being established in more and more countries each year, but interestingly enough for many people who have visited these new tea farms, they've found that they're not always able to buy their product at homegrown prices.

It's led to an increasing desire for people to start their own tea gardens.

Most of the tea gardens in Japan have been around for several generations and the owners have a hard time finding people who are willing to take over the business in order to keep it going.

But there are a lot of young people with dreams of growing their own tea, so they're jumping into the industry head first.

The secret is in their business models—their marketing strategies and their ability to balance quality with affordability are what separate these tea gardens from the rest.

Once you've planted the tea tree, it takes years before it starts producing flowers and leaves that you can sell as tea. During this time, the farmer will have to nourish his plants with fertilizer and pesticides which will cost him a lot of money.

This is why the majority of tea gardens are more interested in developing a source of consistent income than they are about the prices they'll get for their tea. They sell their tea at very reasonable prices in general, and many offer discounts to tourists and people who visit their farms.

This offers a great opportunity to travelers who want to support local businesses and drink some really good tea at the same time. The benefits for tea lovers and farmers alike make this market-based approach an intelligent way to get more people involved in the industry.

In addition, you'll find that the majority of these tea gardens are located in very beautiful places.

These plantations are usually located in rural areas where people can see the tea trees growing alongside other crops that go into making their final products, such as barley and rice.

The owners rely on visits by people like you to make it through the uncertain times that come during years of development, and they do everything they can to make sure you have a great time while visiting their farms.

Many tea gardens claim that they can provide you with the best tea in the country. Others have their own specialty products and many of them are willing to work with you to find teas that will satisfy your unique tastes.

They're experts in growing their product and they are dedicated, not only to providing you with well-rounded products but also to keeping the culture alive that has produced it all this time.

If you're looking for "the tea that is the best in the country", look no further than Japan.

The visit will be a memorable and wonderful experience and you'll definitely come home with some great cups of tea to enjoy every day.

You can always rely on a Tea Hotel to provide you with an exceptional experience and the best possible tea imaginable.

It's a great way to support the farmers and the environment and you'll certainly find that they have more to offer than most other hotels.

We also have many Tea Events in Japan, so look for a "Tea-filled" experience in this amazing country.

CHALLENGES

Tea gardens are still a very new market to the mass consumer market, so there's a lot of room for growth and development. The difference in prices between tea from different countries can be huge since China is so well known around the world for high-quality tea that they're almost always more expensive than others.

One of the most common problems with tea gardens is that they don't have enough demand to guarantee their prices will stay at a certain level. By importing tea from other countries, they're lowering their prices and making it harder to keep them at a level that the local market would accept.

Tea is still experimental for many farmers—they don't always have the same success rate as suppliers in other countries, and people who start selling tea in the US need to be sure that their products will sell globally.

SOLUTION

Like many other companies facing this challenge, these tea gardens are doing their best to balance quality with affordability by establishing relationships with other similar operations.

By working together, they can reduce transportation costs which will make it easier for their products to compete globally.

By setting up a tea garden in a country where demand for high-quality tea far exceeds their supply, they'll be able to generate enough money to meet their living costs while they push to get their product onto the global market.

GETTING STARTED

Tea gardens have only been established in China and Vietnam so far. But with the popularity of fine teas growing around the world each year, other tea-producing countries are starting to realize that planting more tea trees is the way to guarantee that they'll be able to sell their products.

AMERICAN TEA GROWERS

There are many different reasons why you may be interested in growing your own tea. You may want to grow organic teas that are free of the pesticides and herbicides that commercial production uses. Or you might want to try your hand at a new career. Whatever the reason, we have included some basic information about how to grow and process tea on a small scale that applies to home gardeners, as well as some links for those who would like more information about this rewarding career path.

There are different growing locations you may want to consider, such as Hawaii, New York, South Carolina, and Florida which are currently considered the major tea-producing states in the United States.

Growers in these states cultivate a majority of black teas such as English Breakfast and Assam, while green teas are primarily produced in California and Oregon. White teas come primarily from California, with some production also being done in Oregon and Arizona. Oolong teas are cultivated in Oregon and North Carolina.

Planting, growing, and harvesting tea typically follows a standard process throughout the country. The planting season begins from December through March when the soil has warmed. The first step is to dig up or prepare the land for planting, and then add a rich organic material (animal manure) to the soil. Next, layout rows for your plants with the help of a surveyor's chain, ensuring you space each row 6 ft. apart from one another. Once the rows are laid out, you can plant your tea seed in the ground.

For home growers, the seed is a viable option for planting. At this point, you can add some compost or manure to ensure a fertile environment around the seeds, which typically will only take two or three weeks to germinate. Seeds can be bought from local retailers who specialize in tea growing supplies and harvested green teas are also a viable option for planting.

Once the plants are mature enough to be transplanted, you can move them from the fields to a greenhouse or shade house. After a couple of weeks in your shade house, the plants are ready for transplanting again. Tea is typically planted near the top of the ground and can reach as high as 9 ft. tall. Once they are transplanted again, ensure that you space them 2 ft. apart from one another to allow ample room for growth and development.

In the next month, you will see the appearance of plants sprouting. In order to control weeds, sometimes most are removed and others are allowed to grow. After two or three months it is time to begin harvesting tea. It is recommended to harvest for one or two days in order to increase the flavor and aroma of each cup. Tea plants can be harvested for between 20–60 days depending on the variety of tea plants.

Harvesting is done by clipping the top of the plant off. After you have harvested your tea, you can either sell it fresh or process it into a dried product. There are multiple ways to dry the leaves, including laying them out

in the sun or using a dehydrator. Some types of tea leaves can be dry without withering but this is typically reserved for specialty teas such as Japanese green teas.

As you can see, it is not a difficult process to grow your own tea. If you have a green thumb or are interested in starting your own business, this is a rewarding career option that is sure to help you stand out from the crowd.

Once you have harvested tea leaves you must also implement an effective package design for your product. One of the primary components of growing your own tea is also to consider how you are going to sell it. First off, you need to decide whether you are going to sell the tea in loose leaf or bagged form. You can also choose between flavored teas such as herbs and spices or unsweetened teas which are best when used for black teas such as English breakfast and Herbal tea.

Once you have picked a package design, it is vital that you provide your customers with a quality product that they can trust. This means having a quality tea that is organic and free of pesticides, chemicals, or herbicides. It is also important to pick a design that will be sure to stand out on store shelves.

Chapter - 16
GIFT IDEAS FOR FRIENDS

If you're searching for the perfect plant for a friend, look no further than tea plants. Tea is one of the most popular beverages in the world and a great choice to get someone excited about gardening. If you want to give a gift that is low maintenance, a tea plant will provide beauty and enjoyment for your friend year-round.

These are the gift ideas for keeping a tea plant:

• A tea plant in a beautiful pot or trellis that will look great on a patio or deck.

• A few varieties of tea plants will provide a lovely display on the patio.

• A variety of herbal teas to brew with the fresh leaves off your own tea plant.

THE TEA PLANT IN A POT

If you want to give a loved one the gift of tea, but you don't have much gardening space yourself, then a tea plant in a pot is the ideal choice. Most teas prefer well-drained soil, so if it is not already present in your friend's garden, be sure to add some. Buy an attractive pot and fill it with topsoil and organic compost mix with plenty of peat moss. Tuck the plant in and water thoroughly. If possible, also give your friend a few herbal tea varieties to brew with the leaves.

The best varieties for a tea plant in a pot:

• Red rooibos (aspalathus linearis) is an attractive variety that produces lovely red new growth in spring and summer. This variety is grown in South Africa and needs afternoon shade. It can withstand some frost during the winter months if the soil is well mulched.

• White rooibos (aspalathus linearis) grows from 2–4 ft. tall and produces pale white flowers in summer. A beautiful variety that is drought tolerant once established.

- Green rooibos (aspalathus linearis) has attractive glossy green leaves and produces yellow flowers in the summer months. It needs to be planted in partial shade and protected from frost.

- Strawberry oolong (fragrant wenyonii) is a vigorous variety that produces sweet-smelling flowers in the spring. It is deciduous and will lose its leaves in winter.

For a gift that keeps on giving, purchase a few varieties of herbal tea. This will provide your friend with enjoyment throughout the year as they brew themselves a cup of fresh tea leaves at any time. Here are some teas to consider:

- **Red rose petals.** A lovely flower that is perfect for Valentine's Day. They have a gentle flavor with hints of berries.

- **Chamomile.** This popular variety brews to a light golden color and has a soothing, fruity aroma.

- **Orange spice.** The flowers of the orange blossom plant are picked before sunrise and then dried to produce this delicate tea with a sweet hint of citrus.

- **Turmeric.** This popular Asian spice is known for its antioxidant properties and antibiotic properties. It grows to about one foot in height if planted in full sun.

- **Passionflower.** Another durable perennial, the flowers of this variety are edible and make a lovely tea with a sweet, lemony flavor.

- **Wild cherry.** A great tea for those with kidney problems, it is also said to soothe skin rashes, mouth sores, and bee stings (where applicable). The leaves are used as a dye as well.

- **Chamomile variegated variety.** This variety produces lovely pale pink flowers and makes a wonderful tea.

Be sure to offer the gift of tea leaves in a reusable container.

Chapter - 17
HERBAL TEAS FOR HEADACHES

A delicious way to relax and reduce headaches is to create herbal tea blends. Herbs can be brewed into a hot drink or steeped in water and served chilled. Tension headaches can often be relieved by ribwort, skullcap, peppermint, rosemary, or lavender.

I have an aunt who is suffering extremely from migraines. She has tried all sorts of medications, but nothing worked. A close friend of mine recently told me about her grandmother who used to drink a cup of tea before bed every night and had amazing results—she often slept through the night with minimal pain. I thought, why not? We've heard so many positive things about herbal tea and at least giving it a try isn't very expensive.

PEPPERMINT TEA

The smell of this tea wafted through my nose as I soaked in every moment of that experience. There are many health benefits to drinking this deep green brew and it can be found just about anywhere throughout the world.

Ingredients:

- 7 g. fresh peppermint leaves

- 150 g. fresh cucumber

- A few drops of lemon juice

Directions:

1. Wash fresh peppermint leaves and cucumber.

2. Put the ingredients into the blender and mix well.

3. Pour into a clean bottle.

4. The tea is ready!

Drink it all through the day, adding a few drops of lemon juice or honey for taste. This recipe can be applied in case of headache and migraine symptoms when you feel a tension pain that goes right up to your forehead.

ROSEMARY TEA

I love to sit and sip on a hot cup of tea in the evenings. I've heard that Rosemary is a good herb for your health and I am eager to try this out.

Ingredients:

*   7 g. fresh rosemary

*   7 g. fresh mint

*   A few drops of lemon juice

Directions:

1.   Wash fresh rosemary and mint.

2.   Put all the ingredients into the blender and mix well.

3.   Pour into a clean bottle.

4.   The tea is ready!

Drink it throughout the day, adding a few drops of lemon juice or honey for taste. This recipe can be applied in case of headache and migraine symptoms when you feel a tension pain that goes right up to your forehead.

ROSEMARY & LAVENDER TONIC

This recipe is so simple and could be used as a body or hair rinse. "Lavender flowers are renowned for their anti-inflammatory and pain-relieving properties. Rosemary helps to revitalize the mind, while peppermint soothes an aching stomach."

Ingredients:

•   5 g. fresh rosemary

•   5 g. fresh lavender

•   A few drops of lemon juice

Directions:

1.   Wash fresh rosemary and lavender, then add the ingredients to the blender and mix well.

2.   Pour into a clean bottle.

3.   The tea is ready!

Drink it throughout the day, adding a few drops of lemon juice or honey for taste. This recipe can be applied in case of headache and migraine symptoms when you feel a tension pain that goes right up to your forehead.

HERBAL TEA FOR MIGRAINE

Ingredients:

- 3 g. fresh grass

- 7 g. fresh orange

- 4 g. fresh lemon

- 5 g. mint leaves

- 3 g. tarragon

Directions:

1. Put in a blender and blend until smooth.

2. Add a little water, mix well and pour into a clean bottle.

3. The tea is ready!

Consume it throughout the day, adding a few drops of lemon juice or honey for taste. This recipe can be applied in case of headache and migraine symptoms when you feel a tension pain that goes right up to your forehead.

LAVANILLA TONIC

Ingredients:

- 5 g. fresh lavender

- 2–3 pieces of grapes

- 7 g. fresh mint

- Lemon juice of 1 lemon

Directions:

1. Wash fresh lavender and grapes, then add the ingredients to the blender and mix well.

2. Pour into a clean bottle.

3. The tea is ready!

Consume it throughout the day, adding a few drops of lemon juice or honey for taste.

Chapter - 18
HERBAL TEAS FOR HANGOVER RELIEF

DANDELION TONIC

Ingredients:

- 3 g. fresh dandelion

- Lemon juice of 1 lemon

Directions:

1. Wash fresh dandelion, then add the ingredients to the blender and mix well.

2. Pour into a clean bottle.

3. The tea is ready!

Drink it throughout the day, adding a few drops of lemon juice or honey for taste. This recipe can be applied in case of headache and migraine symptoms when you feel a tension pain that goes right up to your forehead.

MINT TEA

Ingredients:

- 2 g. fresh mint leaves

- 200 ml. apple juice, freshly extracted

Directions:

1. Wash the fresh mint leaves well, then add to a blender and mix well.

2. Pour into a clean bottle and add apple juice; stir it gently, cover it, and leave it in the refrigerator for 12 hours.

The next day you can drink the beverage. You can drink a glass of it for headaches, neck pain, or any kind of pain. This recipe is very useful in case of nervousness and stress.

BASIL TEA

Ingredients:

- 4 g. fresh basil

- 2 tbsps. lemon juice

- 2 tsps. honey

Directions:

1. Wash the fresh basil well, then add to the blender and mix well with lemon juice; add honey and blend again.

2. Pour into a clean bottle, cover, and leave it in the refrigerator for 12 hours.

Drink a glass of this recipe for headaches, stiff neck, pain in the shoulder and back, muscle strain, or fatigue. Basil is ideal for those who are prone to stress and anxiety as well.

HERBAL TEA "DYNAMITE"

Ingredients:

- 150 g. elderberry fruit

- 5 g. dried orange peel

- 5 g. rhubarb root

Directions:

1. Wash the elderberry fruit and cut it into a bowl with a knife.

2. Add to the juice of dried orange peel, then add rhubarb root and stir well.

3. Leave it in the refrigerator for 12 hours.

Drink this tea regularly for nervous and stress disorders, headaches, or muscle tightness. (This recipe can be used when you have flu symptoms).

Chapter - 19
HERBAL TEAS FOR COLDS AND ASTHMA

SAGE TEA

Ingredients:

- 2 g. fresh sage

- 200 ml. apple juice, freshly extracted

Directions:

1. Wash the fresh sage well, then add to the blender and mix with apple juice; stir it gently.

2. Pour into a clean bottle and leave it in the refrigerator for 12 hours.

The next day you could drink this tea regularly for colds, hay fever, coughs, or asthma! This recipe is very useful when you have flu symptoms and sneezing is intense.

CINNAMON TEA

Ingredients:

- 4 g. fresh cinnamon

- 2 tbsps. lemon juice

- 2 tsps. honey

Directions:

1. Wash the fresh cinnamon well, then add to a blender and mix well with lemon and honey.

2. Pour into a clean bottle, cover, and leave it in the refrigerator for 12 hours.

The next day you could drink this tea regularly for colds or fever. This recipe is very useful when you have flu symptoms and sneezing is intense.

LICORICE AND APPLE TEA

Ingredients:

- 3 g. fresh licorice

- 200 ml. apple juice, freshly extracted

Directions:

1. Wash the fresh licorice well, then add to the blender and mix with apple juice; stir it gently.

2. Pour into a clean bottle and leave it in the refrigerator for 12 hours.

The next day you could drink this tea regularly for colds or fever. This recipe is very useful when you have flu symptoms and sneezing is intense.

CHAMOMILE TEA

Ingredients:

- 3 g. fresh chamomile

- 2 tbsps. lemon juice

- 2 tsps. honey

Directions:

1. Wash the fresh chamomile well, then add to a blender and mix with lemon juice.

2. Pour into a clean bottle and leave it in the refrigerator for 12 hours.

The next day you may drink this tea regularly for colds or fever. This recipe is very useful when you have flu symptoms and sneezing is intense.

HOPS TEA

Ingredients:

- 2 g. fresh hops

- 200 ml. kerafruit juice

- 2 tsps. honey

Directions:

1. Wash fresh hops, then add to a blender and mix well with the kerafruit juice; stir it gently.

2. Pour into a clean bottle and leave it in the refrigerator for 12 hours.

The next day you may drink this tea regularly for colds or fever. This recipe is very useful when you have flu symptoms and sneezing is intense.

TEA FOR SLEEP

Ingredients:

- 3 g. fresh chamomile

- 5 g. dried orange peel

- 5 g. rhubarb root

Directions:

1. Wash fresh chamomile well, then add to the blender and mix with dried orange peel; add rhubarb root and stir well.

2. Pour into a clean bottle, cover, and leave it in the refrigerator for 12 hours.

The next day you may drink this tea regularly for sleep disorders! This recipe is very useful when you have flu symptoms and sneezing is intense.

CHAMOMILE TEA WITH HONEY

Ingredients:

- 3 g. fresh chamomile

- 2 tsps. honey

Directions:

1. Wash the fresh chamomile well, then add to the blender and mix well with honey.

2. Pour into a clean bottle and leave it in the refrigerator for 12 hours.

The next day you may drink this tea regularly for colds or fever. This recipe is very useful when you have flu symptoms and sneezing is intense.

CHAMOMILE TEA WITH GINGER

Ingredients:

- 3 g. fresh chamomile

- 2 g. ginger

- 2 tsps. honey

Directions:

1. Wash the fresh chamomile well, then add to the blender and mix with ginger; stir it gently.

2. Pour into a clean bottle and leave it in the refrigerator for 12 hours.

The next day you can drink this tea regularly for colds or fever. This recipe is very useful when you have flu symptoms and sneezing is intense.

ORANGE PEEL TEA

Ingredients:

- 5 g. dried orange peel

- 5 g. rhubarb root

Directions:

1. Wash the dried orange peel well, then add to a blender and mix with rhubarb root.

2. Pour into a clean bottle and leave it in the refrigerator for 12 hours.

The next day you can drink this tea regularly for sleep disorders! This recipe is very useful when you have flu symptoms and sneezing is intense.

Chapter - 20
BOOST IMMUNITY TEA

SOUR FRUIT TEA

Ingredients:

- 6 g. watermelon

- 2 g. grape

- 1 tbsp. apple juice

Directions:

1. Cut the watermelon into small pieces, remove seeds; add grape and apple juice in a blender, mix carefully to get a rich pink drink.

2. Mix watermelon, grape, and apple juice in a blender and mix well. Pour into a clean bottle and leave it in the refrigerator for 12 hours.

You can drink this tea regularly for weak immunity, cough, diarrhea, and muscle tension! This fruit tea is good for people who eat frequently fatty foods or don't have enough fruit intake in their diet.

LEMONGRASS TEA

Ingredients:

- Lemongrass

- Grinded ginger

- 1 tsp. sugar (optional)

- Water

Directions:

1.   Bring water to a boil. Add the lemongrass and grinded ginger.

2.   Cover for 5 minutes, strain, add sugar if desired.

3.   Serve hot or cold.

4.   Keeps 10 days in the fridge or 2 weeks in the freezer.

TURMERIC TEA

Ingredients:

- 1 tbsp. turmeric powder

- 1 tsp. sugar

- Salt to taste (optional)

Directions:

1.   Boil water; add turmeric powder, salt, and sugar.

2.   Strain after 10 minutes.

3.   Serve hot with honey.

4.   Keep in the fridge for 3 days.

Turmeric is a wonderful spice to reduce inflammation and cure a variety of ailments.

GINGER TEA WITH HONEY

Ingredients:

- 1 tsp. ginger powder

- 2 tsps. sugar (optional)

- Honey to taste (optional)

Directions:

1. Boil water; add ginger powder, sugar, and honey.

2. Strain after 5 minutes.

3. Serve hot or cold with honey.

4. Keeps in the fridge for 3 days.

Turmeric and ginger are a combination I like very much. I use it more than once a day.

LEMON TEA WITH HONEY AND ALMOND MILK

Ingredients:

- 1 tsp. lemon juice

- 1 tbsp. honey (optional)

- Almond milk to taste (optional)

Directions:

1. Boil water, add the lemon juice.

2. Cover for 10 minutes.

3. Add honey to taste, mix well.

4. Add a dash of almond milk if desired.

5. Let cool before drinking.

6. Keeps in the fridge for 5 days.

Serve it as a refreshing drink or as a beverage in its own right. Make sure to keep it dry and if you keep it in the fridge, do not let the bottle touch any surfaces or reach up to the milk.

Chapter - 21
TEA FOR STOMACH PROBLEMS

FENNEL TEA

Ingredients:

- 200 g. fennel leaves

- 1 tsp. dried thyme

- 3 c. boiling water

- 1 tsp. of dried ginger root

Directions:

1. Grind the leaves and thyme in a coffee grinder until it is fine and put in a teapot.

2. Pour the water and add 1 tsp. of dried ginger root (also make the sandogura).

3. Boil 10 minutes, turn off the fire, cover, wait for 10 more minutes and blend it with a blender until smooth.

4. Drink up to 1 glass a day, preferable after meals.

CARROT AND GINGER TEA

Ingredients:

- 1 ½ lb. fresh carrots (about 5 carrots)

- 3 tbsps. ginger root

- 1 c. milk

- Honey

Directions:

1. Add grated carrot and grated ginger root in a blender, mix it well until it becomes fine powder then add milk in the blender and turn on the fire.

2. Boil for 10 minutes on medium-low heat and cook for 10 more minutes on low heat.

3. Strain the tea after it has boiled and add honey, mix well.

Drink 1 cup of this tea every morning to improve the digestion system and relieve stomach problems.

LICORICE TEA

Ingredients:

- 100 g. licorice root

- 2 c. water

Directions:

1. Cut the licorice root into small pieces and put it in a pot, pour the water.

2. Boil for 10 minutes.

3. Turn off the fire and leave it covered for 10 minutes more, then strain the tea through a filter.

You should take 1 cup of this tea several times a day, preferable before meals.

FENNEL TEA WITH MILK AND HONEY

Ingredients:

- 100 g. fennel
- ½ c. milk
- Honey (as needed)

Directions:

1. Boil the fennel root with water for 15 minutes, then strain the tea.

2. Add milk and honey to the tea and stir it well.

Drink this tea regularly in case of ulcers, constipation, or indigestion.

LICORICE TEA WITH MILK AND CANE SUGAR

Ingredients:

- 250 ml. licorice tea
- 500 ml. milk
- 100 g. cane sugar

Directions:

1. Boil licorice root with water for 15 minutes, then strain the tea and let it cool down.

2. Add milk and cane sugar to the tea and stir it well.

Drink this tea regularly in case of ulcers, constipation, or indigestion.

Chapter - 22
DIVERSE PLANTS THAT MAKE GREAT TEA

1. **Rugosa rose:** It's very difficult to grow tea from the flowers or fruit, but you can make use of the leaves.

2. **Guayusa leaves:** This plant has caffeine content comparable to coffee and a smoother taste than tea made with roasted leaves (such as most black teas).

3. **Jasmine flower**: This flower is frequently used in Chinese green tea blends, and its flavor is sweet, delicate, and complex. Jasmine flowers make a flavorful brew that can be drunk both hot and cold.

4. **Passionflower:** This shrub has an exotic spicy flavor that's pungent, sweet, and grassy.

5. **Calendula (calendula officinalis):** This is now used as a cure for stabbing pains or cramps. It's also used to relieve inflammation and promote wound healing.

6. **Lemon balm:** Another perennial herb with lemon-scented leaves that bring a light bitter note to tea blends; the flower buds are used for flavoring herbal teas and are also used in cooking and perfume making.

7. **Lavender:** This herb has a distinctive, refreshing flavor and has been used in teas since the 1800s.

8. **Elderflower:** A mildly fruity flower that makes a fragrant tea with light astringency, rich flavor, and delicate aroma.

9. **Yerba mate leaves:** This South American plant has a strong, woodsy flavor with hints of citrus and berries; it's often used as an herbal tea for stamina and energy.

10. **Bilberry leaf (vaccinium myrtillus):** Is often used in teas and extracts for vision problems like macular degeneration and night blindness.

11. **Rose hips:** These are the red fruits of the European rose and make an excellent tea in their own right; they also impart their flavor to other teas (for example, Chinese hibiscus).

12. **Peppermint:** This perennial herb is often used in refreshing, bright herbal teas with a flavor that's cool, minty, and bitter.

13. **Bergamot:** This is the fruit of the small aromatic evergreen shrub native to Asia (also known as orange mint or mandarin flower); it's a strongly flavored herb that makes a tea with a complex but balanced flavor reminiscent of citrus fruit and berries.

14. **Chamomile flower:** This is the flower of the wild daisy native to Asia (also known as Roman chamomile); flavoring tea with strong floral notes, it can be used to help ease nerves or insomnia and is also used in many herbal teas.

15. **Rose petals:** This flower contains pungent oil that makes a fragrant tea with an interesting flavor and aroma reminiscent of violet flowers (also known as roschip).

16. **Safflower flowers:** They contain a strong yellow pigment that can be used to make yellow tea.

17. **Forsythia (forsythia suspensa):** Has a sweet taste, so it's often used in herbal teas as a sweetener (but keep in mind that you won't get all the nutritional benefits without eating the fruit or tea leaves).

18. **Hibiscus (hibiscus esculentus):** This is used topically for bruises and cuts. It is also used for herb tea to treat urinary tract infections, as it helps to increase bladder output and decrease pain.

19. **Orange peel:** This is the fruit of the fragrant tropical tree (also known as bigarade); it offers a full, bitter-sweet flavor and makes a fantastic tea with notes of citrus fruit.

20. **Rose flower:** This is the fruit of the rose shrub, which has a unique sweet floral flavor; it also makes a hearty tea.

21. **Hops cones:** These are the fruit of the hop vine, used to produce beer and flavor tea; they impart a rich, bitter taste to the tea.

22. **Pineapple flower buds:** This is the bud of the tropical pineapple (also known as fragrant pineapple); it's sometimes used in herbal teas instead of or alongside its leaves and fruit.

23. **Cinnamon leaf:** This is the leaf of the tropical evergreen tree (also known as cassia); it has a warm, spicy flavor with mild astringency and makes a fragrant tea.

24. **Sassafras root bark:** This is the root of the tree native to North America (also known as sassafras); it's occasionally harvested for its aromatic oil and medicinal value.

25. **Aloe vera:** (Aloe barbadensis) sprays are now used to help heal burns. It's used topically and in a tea to soothe stomach pain, treat intestinal problems, treat conjunctivitis, reduce inflammation (including of the pancreas), and reduce breast pain.

26. **Eucalyptus leaves:** This herb has an odor that's reminiscent of menthol and chamomile and is sometimes used in herbal teas to help ease respiratory issues.

27. **Lemon verbena:** This herb has a warm, mildly citrus flavor with sweet floral undertones; it's sometimes used as an herbal tea or in aromatherapy.

28. **Ginger root:** This is the root of the perennial plant native to Asia (also known as zingiber); it has a spicy, vegetal flavor with a slight citrus aroma.

29. **Blackberry leaf (rubus fruticosus):** This is often used for diarrhea and to help soothe an upset stomach.

30. **Parsley seed:** This herb has strong flavors reminiscent of peppermint, rosemary, and thyme; it's often used in herbal teas and for garnish on foods.

31. **Lemon balm leaves:** This herb has a floral, sweet flavor that's sometimes used in herbal teas and aromatherapy for its antidepressant effects.

32. **Sage leaves:** This is the herb cultivated from the wild plant native to Europe (also known as sweet sage); it offers a strong, woody flavor with an astringent, slightly bitter aftertaste.

33. **Chicory root:** This is the root of the plant native to Europe (also known as endive or curly endive); it has a potato-like flavor with notes of cooked vegetables and makes an excellent herbal tea.

34. **Comfrey root:** This herb is the root of the plant native to Europe (also known as knitbone and motherwort); it has a strong, bitter taste and is occasionally used in herbal teas.

35. **Echinacea herb:** This herb has an odor that's reminiscent of mint and citrus and is sometimes used in herbal teas to boost the immune system.

36. **Apple geranium leaves:** This herb is cultivated from a wild plant native to Africa; it has a mild, sweet flavor.

37. **Rose geranium leaves:** This herb is cultivated from the wild plant native to the Mediterranean; it has a strong, sweet flavor with a hint of citrus and spice.

38. **Lemon verbena leaves:** This herb is cultivated from the wild plant native to South America; it has a minty, lemon flavor and may be used in herbal teas or as an ingredient in desserts.

39. **Fennel seeds:** This herb has an aroma that's reminiscent of licorice and anise and is sometimes used in herbal teas for digestive purposes.

40. **Angelica root:** This herb has a peppery, onion-like flavor and is sometimes used in herbal teas to stimulate the digestive tract or to ease diarrhea.

41. **Anise seeds:** This herb has an aroma that's reminiscent of licorice and is sometimes used in herbal teas for digestive purposes.

42. **Milk thorn:** This herb is native to Africa and has an aroma reminiscent of licorice; it contains bitters that help to relieve intestinal gas.

43. **Figs:** These are the fruit of certain trees in the genus Ficus; they taste subtly sweet and taste just as good raw as they do roasted, or used in desserts. They contain a lot of fiber and are packed with vitamins such as vitamin C and vitamin A, as well as various minerals like potassium and iron.

44. **Milk thistle:** Contains antioxidants and is also claimed to help with various liver issues. The herb is used in herbal medicine for people and animals.

45. **Mullein (verbascum thapsus):** Helps with coughs and colds, as well as earaches, inflammation, and laryngitis. It can be used topically or in a tea for these conditions.

46. **Fragrant bergamot flower (citrus aurantium bergamia):** This is used in herbal medicine for congestion, indigestion, and headache.

CONCLUSION

If you have space and time to do so, growing your own tea garden can be a fulfilling and rewarding experience, with plenty of funny stories for anyone who loves to chat. If you're wondering how to get started with it, we've created this book full of helpful tips and tricks.

To grow your own tea garden, you need space, a steady supply of water and fertilizer, and an area that's free from pests and disease. You also need plenty of new plants, as well as the know-how to care for them.

If your area is large enough and suitable to grow tea trees, then you can add an area around them to create a better microclimate and optimize the weather. You'll need a garden bench to sit on to tend your tea plants, and you'll also need a compost bin.

It is possible to grow a variety of tea types on a small scale… but it takes determination. You can't just jump into it and expect tea to come running! Then again, if you're looking for something that'll make you feel like you've done something productive while you're off at work or on vacation, then growing your own tea leaves is the perfect job.

If you're wondering how much space your tea plants will take up, we suggest that you start with a small planter and see just how big it will get. You may be surprised to see that even an eight-foot-tall tree can fit into something much smaller.

You need to water your plants regularly. If you're using a drip system, it should be set up to water the plants in the morning or evening. Once a week is plenty of time for the tea trees to get their fill of water. Sprinklers should be used to water your plants about once a day.

If you're trying to grow your tea tree for sale, then you need to make sure that it develops a good leaf and looks appealing. To do so, try training the branches to grow in certain shapes. You can also trim the buds on the top of the tree to make it unique and attractive.

Thank you for reading till the end! I hope this book is helpful for you, and make sure to share it with your tea lovers!

Made in United States
Orlando, FL
11 December 2022

26153301R00063